ENLIGHTENED WITHIN

A True Story About a Family That Lived in a Haunted House

Wendie Willis

Copyright © 2015 Wendie Willis.

All rights reserved. No part of this book may be used or reproduced by any means, graphic, electronic, or mechanical, including photocopying, recording, taping or by any information storage retrieval system without the written permission of the publisher except in the case of brief quotations embodied in critical articles and reviews.

LifeRich Publishing is a registered trademark of
The Reader's Digest Association, Inc.

LifeRich Publishing books may be ordered through booksellers or by contacting:

LifeRich Publishing
1663 Liberty Drive
Bloomington, IN 47403
www.liferichpublishing.com
1 (888) 238-8637

Because of the dynamic nature of the Internet, any web addresses or links contained in this book may have changed since publication and may no longer be valid. The views expressed in this work are solely those of the author and do not necessarily reflect the views of the publisher, and the publisher hereby disclaims any responsibility for them.

Any people depicted in stock imagery provided by Thinkstock are models, and such images are being used for illustrative purposes only. Certain stock imagery © Thinkstock.

ISBN: 978-1-4897-0373-6 (sc)
ISBN: 978-1-4897-0372-9 (hc)
ISBN: 978-1-4897-0374-3 (e)

Library of Congress Control Number: 2014921501

Print information available on the last page.

LifeRich Publishing rev. date: 3/3/2015

Contents

Preface vii
Introduction xi

Chapter I   Courtship 1
Chapter II   Building a Relationship 12
Chapter III   The Ex's Meet 24
Chapter IV   Marriage 28
Chapter V   First Year 36
Chapter VI   Second Year 45
Chapter VII   Third Year 51
Chapter VIII Fourth Year 86
Chapter IX   New House 139

Epilogue 155

Preface

This book would not have been written without receiving the message from God to write it.

There are a lot of true stories about evil spirits or hauntings and many times people don't know what to do in a situation like that. They think people won't believe them or that they're crazy. Often they will lean on "mediums' or "psychics" for assistance and some kind of message. This is what God tells us in Leviticus 19:31 "Do not turn to mediums or seek out spiritists, for you will be defiled by them. I am the Lord your God." It's really important that we turn to God for help and not the things of this world, for those things are not of God. They will only distract and clutter your mind and soul even more. God has given me a gift and I plan on using it to help others in their battles. We are all in some kind of battle and if we have the proper tools, we can overcome them. Ephesians 6:12 "For our struggle is not against flesh and blood, but against the rulers, against the authorities, against the powers of this dark world and against the spiritual forces of evil within the heavenly realms."

I have been blessed with a wonderful, loving family that has supported me throughout the whole process of writing. Thank you for all of your encouragement and patience. My love goes to my husband, Jay, and our four amazing children, Brittney, Nick, Josh and Tyler.

I would also like to thank my mom and all of my siblings for their support and prayers during and after our experience.

INTRODUCTION

It all started back in the summer of 2002… planning a wedding and joining two families together. Penelope and Richard had been married before and have three children between the two of them, Cassandra eight, Casey six, and Richard's son, Michael, who is also six. Much to their surprise, the challenge wasn't blending two families together, but what they were to discover within their home. They were not alone…

Psalm 91

He who dwells in the shelter of the most high will rest in the shadow of the Almighty. I will say of the Lord, "He is my refuge and my fortress, my God, in whom I trust." Surely he will save you from the fowler's snare and from the deadly pestilence. He will cover you with his feathers, and under his wings you will find refuge; his faithfulness will be your shield and rampart. You will not fear the terror of night, nor the arrow that flies by day, nor the pestilence that stalks in the darkness, nor the plague that destroys at midday. A thousand may fall at your side, ten thousand at your right hand, but it will not come near you. You will only observe with your eyes and see the punishment of the wicked. If you make the Most High your dwelling – even the Lord, who is my refuge – then no harm will befall you, no disaster will come near your tent. For he will command his angels concerning you to guard you in all your ways; they will lift you up in their hands, so that you will not strike your foot against a stone. You will tread upon the lion and the cobra; you will trample the great lion and the serpent. "Because he loves me," says the Lord, "I will protect him, for he acknowledges my name. He will call upon me, and I will answer him; I will be with him in trouble, I will deliver him and honor him. With long life will I satisfy him and show him my salvation."

I can do all things through Christ who strengthens me.
Philippians 4:13

COURTSHIP

Five long years had passed since Penelope had become a single mom of two. She owned an adorable Cape Cod home, white with green trim and located in the beautiful Pacific Northwest. Outdoors, it featured an enclosed backyard and play structure. At this point in her life, she'd begun missing a partner and a good father for her children. As it was, her children only saw their dad during the summer months and occasionally throughout the year for holidays.

Penelope mused as she dried the last dish. *God, I need a good husband...a soul mate for myself and a father for Cassandra and Casey.* She promised God to give up dating and let him decide who would be the right person in their lives. It seemed as if dating didn't work well, anyway, without God's hand involved. Penelope did not want to give any commitment or accept it from anyone until she knew without a doubt that God had picked the right man for herself and her children. One year after relinquishing her love life over to God... the story begins.

Penelope woke up one morning just thinking about life and feeling the need to stay in bed and relax. It was a beautiful Sunday morning, which is rare in the Pacific Northwest in November. *I think the kids and I will stay home and not go to church. Yeah, we can just have church here today.* God started speaking to Penelope through her inner spirit… "You need to go to church today," the voice said. Accompanying the voice was a vision: she saw a man who she knew, though she couldn't remember his name. He was a tall man built like a football player, blue eyes, and a dirty blonde spiky haircut. She thought to herself, *Man, is he cute! Hey, he's the one who used to be married to Crystal, the girl I met at the athletic club. We raced in Triathlons.* The voice continued, "You need to go to church. Go to the early service, and you will see why." That was the end of the vision and message. Penelope turned quickly to look at the clock located across the room. It read 8:00 a.m. Church started at 9:00 a.m.! Her heart started racing as she hurried to get dressed. *I need to get the kids up and ready! This is why I didn't want to go; we rush all week long. Sheesh! I just wanted one day to chill out."* Oh, here they come down the stairs now.

"Good morning guys! How did you sleep?"

Wiping her eyes, Cassandra said, "Pretty good, mom."

Bright eyed and bushy tailed, Casey said, "Mom, can we go to church today?"

"Yes, we are going, mister. So you guys need to get dressed while I make breakfast."

God is amazing how he works! Penelope got the kids dressed, fed and out the door by 8:50 a.m., just enough time to get to church and walk in while the singing started. Penelope leaned down toward Cassandra and said, "Since Casey has a hard time sitting still, let's drop him off at his Sunday school class first, and then we'll go find a seat." She and Cassandra walked Casey to his class and as she was signing him in, she thought she would try and locate the name of the man in her vision on the Sunday school check-in list. She skimmed through the list and saw there was a Michael McCallister! She knew that was the child, but his dad's name wasn't signed next to it.

Penelope looked over at Casey and said, "Have fun, sweetheart! See you after church." Casey waved goodbye to his mom and began playing with a dump truck. She and Cassandra walked into the sanctuary. It was crowded. "Cassandra, let's go over to the left side and see if there are any seats."

Cassandra tugged on her mom's dress and said, "No mommy, let's go over this way."

Penelope saw the man that was in her vision sitting on the right side of the sanctuary. Her heart started racing. She almost couldn't believe this was happening. God's gift to her consisted of movie clips that would play in her mind. They would be events that hadn't taken place yet. God instructed her to pray about them or prepare for them. Throughout her life, there had never been a vision that didn't come true. Sometimes it would literally be a day before it happened—other times it might be years.

There were no seats to be found. They had to go sit where Cassandra was pointing, which was just a few pews away from the man in her vision. They finally sat down and Penelope had a perfect view of this man from where they were sitting. *Oh my gosh, is he cute! Thank you, God!* He kind of glanced over, but she couldn't tell if he saw her or not. Penelope tried to focus on the singing, which was her favorite part of the church service. Suddenly it was time for the sermon.

Pastor Frank announced, "It's time for kids to go to their Sunday school classes. Everyone else turn to your neighbor and say, "Hi"; they might just be your next best friend." Penelope was a bit relieved to walk Cassandra to her class and take a breather before she had to walk back into the sanctuary. Any other time, she really enjoyed listening to Pastor Frank, but it was very hard for her to focus after receiving the vision that morning and then glancing over at this guy. *Lord! You're always right, and I am seeing why. Even though I'm sure what I'm thinking right now is not everything you wanted to share with me about this man.*

After a month of going to the early service at church and making herself noticeable to this man, he still had yet to say anything to her. One Sunday evening as Penelope was praying, she said to God, "I don't know what to do. I refuse to ask this guy out and he doesn't seem to notice me at all." She couldn't ignore the feeling she had inside telling her to wait it out a bit longer. The small inner voice speaking to her heart once again always gave her hope.

Meanwhile, over at the man's house, he and his son, Michael, were eating dinner together while listening to Christmas music. It was the Christmas season and they should have been happy, but somehow they couldn't grasp that cheerful spirit. Their doorbell rang. Dad rose from the table to answer the door. He said, "Finish eating your dinner, son."

He opened the door and said, "Well, if it isn't Pastor Frank! What brings you out this way?"

Pastor Frank said, "Hey Richard! I'm just dropping by to say Hi."

"Really Pastor Frank? I didn't think you would just drop by someone's house on Christmas Eve without a reason. Tell me why you came by."

Pastor Frank said, "Ok, ok, there's this girl named Penelope Anderson that goes to our church, and I think she's interested in you.

Richard said, "What? You think she's interested in me?"

"Well, she can't make it any clearer to you, Richard. She has moved her seat closer and closer to you for the past month. If she gets any closer, she'll be sitting in your lap! So I came by to suggest that you take her out for coffee."

Richard stood there for a second and said, "Well, I don't know Frank."

Pastor Frank said, "Just take the girl out for a cup of coffee, Richard!" Pastor Frank left, giving Richard something worthwhile to think about.

Another week went by and it was a rainy Sunday morning. Richard took Michael into Sunday school. "Have fun, Michael, I'll see you after church, bud."

Penelope was dropping Casey off at the same time. Richard and Penelope locked eyes. Penelope's heart was beating fast and she was thinking to herself, finally this guy sees me!

She tried to relax and said in a soft but confident voice, "Good morning."

Richard replied with a "how ya doing" tone, and said, "Good Morning" back. They both went into church and sat in separate pews. That was the one Sunday morning that Penelope felt there was finally a little progress in getting closer to this guy. She didn't even care if he said any more to her that day or not. After church was over and their kids were picked up from class, Pastor Frank handed Richard an umbrella so he could walk Penelope out to her car. She could tell he felt a little awkward but at the same time, he liked it.

During the following week, Penelope was dreaming of this guy. She wondered if he was thinking of her at all. It was Sunday and, once again, she was leaving church without talking to him. Richard came up from behind and tapped Penelope on the head with the church bulletin. She turned around and almost bumped into him. He leaned in slightly toward Penelope and asked, "Would you--would you like to go out tonight and get a pizza?"

Caught off guard, she said, "Tonight?" She was afraid she wouldn't have time to arrange for a babysitter. As Richard stepped closer and looked down upon her, he said, "Well, I was thinking if it's alright with you, we could go out with our kids to Chucky Cheese."

Penelope was relieved, even though her rule was never to take her children with her on dates. Knowing that God was involved, she knew it would be okay. So Richard and Penelope walked out together from church for the very first time and exchanged phone numbers. After she drove off in her car she yelled, "Yes!" She'd finally got his name: Richard! She thought to herself, I would have never guessed his name. Richard called her that afternoon to let her know that he and his son would be by to pick them up at 5:30 p.m.

Right after Penelope hung up the phone, she immediately called her sister-in-law. Marsha answered the phone and Penelope said, "Marsha! You will never believe this!"

Before Marsha could answer, Penelope proceeded to say, "Cassandra, Casey and I are going out with that guy from church and his son tonight!"

Marsha said, "Wow! That's great. So did you finally find out what his name is?"

"Yes, it's Richard."

"Well, I hope everyone has a good time tonight. Call me later and tell me all the details."

"Oh I will. Talk to you later, Marsha."

Five-thirty p.m. could not come any quicker! Richard arrived on time, with his son standing next to him, looking so very cute. Everyone introduced each other and then they headed out to Chucky Cheese. The conversation in the car went well. You could tell that Michael was excited to make new friends with Cassandra and Casey. Upon arriving at Chucky Cheese, the kids took off to play and crawl through the tunnel mazes. The kids hit it off just great. Richard was asking Penelope a lot of questions. After awhile, she was feeling as if she was on the judge's stand. She was thinking that this guy must not have been on a date in a looong time. She finally couldn't take it any longer and said, "You've been asking a lot of questions."

Richard looked embarrassed and said, "Sorry, I guess I'm just not used to this." Feeling bad for him, she reassured Richard that it was ok, they should just relax and enjoy the evening. Everyone sat down and ate pizza and then the kids were off again playing in the maze tunnels having fun.

Richard looked across the table at Penelope and said, "Do you think you would want any more children?"

She could have been asked any question but that one. After having two already and going through a divorce, she did not want any more. A lot of those feelings had to do with raising her two by herself, and she didn't have the confidence that someone would be there for her if she went through that again.

Penelope looked down at the table and said, "Well, I really don't want to have any more, Richard."

With confidence, he said, "Well, you just haven't been with the right person, that's all."

Penelope looked up at him and said, "Well, maybe, but I still feel that way."

Richard said, "Do you think if you were with the right person you would want to?"

She hesitated. "I don't know." She then glanced at her watch and thought, shoot! It's getting late and I have to get up for work early and the kids have school.

"We should probably head out now," she said, "with work and school in the morning."

Disappointed he said, "Ohhh, let's round up our kids and go then, I guess."

As Richard pulled up to Penelope's house they talked for a few minutes. She heard a tapping sound. Penelope looked over at Richard's feet, he was tapping his right foot on the floor like Thumper in the movie, Bambi. Penelope thought that was so darn cute. She could tell he didn't want her to get out of the car yet.

Richard said, "Well, call me sometime."

Call me sometime?

Does that mean he didn't have fun? She didn't know how to take that. She got out of the car and said in the most positive voice she could, "We'll talk soon! We had fun, thanks."

A week went by. Penelope called Marsha again. "Gosh, Marsha, I don't know if Richard had fun or not last weekend. He hasn't called me all week."

Marsha said, "Well, didn't you say he's traveling this week?"

"Yes, but he could have at least called by now."

"Well, maybe he's thinking about it," Marsha said. "Don't worry, if it's meant to be, he will call you."

Later that day, Penelope got up the gumption to call Richard. *Sheesh! What harm will it do, I'll just call and get this over with so we both know where we stand with each other.* She took a deep breath and called Richard's cell phone number.

Richard answered.

"Hi Richard, its Penelope."

Richard cleared his throat and said, "Hey, I'm up in Seattle."

She responded, "You did mention that last week, didn't you? Well, I was just calling to say hi and see how you're doing."

"I'm doing great now."

Penelope had butterflies going off in her stomach. "Well, that's really good to hear."

"Yes, I'm glad you called me, Penelope."

She was thinking she shouldn't have waited so long. They wound up talking for hours on the phone. Finally, Richard said, "How about you and I go out on a real date this weekend?"

Trying to hold back the excitement, Penelope said, "That sounds like a lot of fun."

Richard picked Penelope up the following Friday evening to take her out to the Chart House, which is a very nice seafood restaurant along the Columbia River. The food is spectacular and wine choices are exquisite. They both dressed up very nicely, Richard had tan dress slacks and a plaid blazer that matched. Penelope had a very nice shimmery black dress on. As Richard walked through the door at Penelope's house, he looked at her with eyes of approval. Penelope could easily read his face. *Wow! He really likes what I'm wearing and is attracted to me. Well, the feeling is mutual, my friend.*

On the way to the restaurant, Richard said, "I didn't think that you were going to call. You acted like you wanted to leave early at Chucky Cheese. So I thought you weren't having fun…"

Penelope immediately interjected, "Oh no! I guess I should have made that clear. I was just thinking about having to get up early for work and having the children ready for school the next morning. I had a good time. It was just a little hectic in Chucky Cheese."

Richard said, "Oh, I thought I blew it by asking too many questions." Richard and Penelope just chuckled, happy to be out alone. At the restaurant, they could not stop talking. There was so much to learn from each other and both were so engaged in conversation that it took two hours before they even ordered dinner. The whole evening they locked eyes and wouldn't have cared if the restaurant burned down. They did manage to order oysters on the half-shell. Penelope loved seafood and really wanted to finish the last half-shell, but it was colossal in size. She didn't want to embarrass herself in front of Richard, so it sat there for a long time.

Richard looked at the half-shell and smiled. "Penelope, aren't you going to finish that one? I know you want to eat that."

Penelope kind of laughed and said, "No, that's ok."

Richard said, "C'mon, go ahead and eat it."

Penelope took a deep breath, picked up the shell, and swallowed the oyster whole. When she was done she said, "Now I feel better," and they both laughed.

Richard leaned closer. "Come here, I want to tell you something."

She leaned over and put her ear toward Richard. He leaned in and gave her a kiss on her cheek. Penelope was caught off guard. She really thought he was going to whisper something in her ear.

All Penelope could come up with was, "That was nice, thank you." *Sheesh!! What an idiot! I just messed up his kiss.*

Richard looked over at her and smiled. After a nice bottle of wine and a wonderful dinner, neither of them wanted to go home and pick up the kids. But it was time for them to go, so they headed back to Penelope's house to pick up the children. Upon arriving, they both walked in together. All three children were there with their babysitter, Kelsey. It worked out great to have one babysitter for the evening. Plus the three kids got along so well, it was fun for them. Kelsey said, "The kids were great! We watched a movie, ate popcorn, and then played some games. I hope you don't mind, but since they were really tired, I let them all sleep together downstairs in your bed."

Penelope said, "That's fine, thank you, Kelsey" Kelsey packed up her things and drove herself home.

Penelope then turned to Richard and they walked together toward the stairway that led downstairs. As they were about to go downstairs to check on the children, he pulled Penelope closer to him and this time she knew he wanted to kiss her. Richard tripped on the step and then said, "No one ever said I was Casanova." Penelope laughed and Richard looked at her like he wasn't going to give up, so he pulled her in even closer and this time they kissed on the lips with passion. The fireworks went off in Penelope's mind and she whispered, Thank you, God.

BUILDING A RELATIONSHIP

The next day was Monday, which meant it was another week at the office. She arrived at work and upon her desk stood a beautiful flower arrangement. Surprised, she searched for the card. They were from Richard. Penelope said, "Awww, how sweet."

Penelope immediately called Richard to thank him. He began emailing her at work and calling when he had the chance. She was afraid she would get in trouble because they talked a lot.

A few days later, while on the phone, Penelope said, "Why don't you meet me for lunch today?"

Richard said, "Sure, what time?"

Well, how about around noonish?"

"That sounds great!"

Richard arrived right on time as usual, and was introduced to several people around the office and then off the two went for a nice lunch.

Upon returning, Penelope could not keep Richard out of her thoughts. It was really hard to concentrate on her work. She was thinking like a schoolgirl, imagining what her name would sound like with Richard's surname. Hmmmmm, Penelope

McAllister.... Penelope Lea McAllister...loved the sound of it. It made her heart leap.

It was soon January and Richard invited Penelope and the kids to a Super Bowl party. The party was with his softball friends and their families. Penelope thought this should be a lot of fun and was looking forward to meeting Richard's friends, she just wished the game was on a different night of the week. She had to get up at 5:00 a.m. for work on Mondays. *Ah well, we just won't stay out too late.* Everyone arrived at the party and was introduced. Richard's friend had a huge, beautiful home. It was very airy and spacious, kind of like a modern loft. A lot of other children were running around having fun. Penelope observed that there seemed to be a lot of drinking going on. Obviously, most Super Bowl parties included alcohol, but this wasn't just a few drinks. This crowd was ready to party. She instantly thought, uh oh, this brings back too many memories of my ex-husband. Her ex used to go out with friends all during the week and stay out until the wee hours of the morning. Sometimes he came home and other times he didn't, but she kept an open mind and tried to be positive. Meanwhile, Casey, Cassandra and Michael were having a blast with the other kids. Penelope checked on the kids every once in awhile and then went back to the room where the adults hung out watching the game. Richard was happy to see her every time she came back into the room. The two of them had a very strong magnetic attraction that seemed to be unstoppable. They stood very close to each other during the whole game. As Penelope gazed across the room, she noticed that one of the women who wasn't with anyone kept looking at them. It was a resentful stare. She leaned over to Richard and whispered about the woman in his ear. Richard looked over at the girl and then she looked away. He whispered that she used to have a crush on him, but he was never interested. Penelope kind of chuckled inside and said, "Well, I think she's still interested by the way she keeps looking over here."

Richard put his arm around Penelope to reassure her she had nothing to worry about. The look on Richard's face was intense as he stared into Penelope's eyes. She could feel and see his love for her for the very first time.

Finally, it was time to round up the kids and head home. Casey and Cassandra appeared tired and Penelope felt bad because they were going to be even more tired in the morning. It was 11:00 p.m. before they got home. As they were driving home, Penelope had to ask Richard, "Does that group usually get together like that on the weekends?"

Richard hesitated in his reply, which meant she wasn't going to like his answer. "Yes, they do, but I only hang out with them during softball season."

Penelope said, "Riiiight."

Richard got a bit defensive. "No, really, I try to limit my time spent with them for that very reason."

Penelope opened up and told Richard about her ex-husband and why she was sensitive about the topic. She also made it very clear that if this is what Richard wanted to do with his friends, ok, but she didn't want anything to do with that sort of lifestyle. She felt like a panther that needed to protect her cubs. She really didn't want to endeavor another relationship with someone who wanted to party every weekend. But, most importantly, she'd promised herself that Casey and Cassandra would never be exposed to that environment ever again. After all, she did move all the way from the East Coast to the West Coast to gain some peace and relief from their prior situation.

Richard said, "I hope you had a good time?"

"Oh, I did and your friends are very nice; I just can't be involved in another relationship where people are out drinking every weekend. Every once in awhile is okay, but I'm just not into the 'party' scene anymore. Meaning, I know this is not where God wants me or my children."

"Do you think about that with your son?" Richard replied. "I do and, as you can tell, I don't go out with them a lot. Trust me; this is not what I want to be doing every weekend either. I really want to settle down with a family and enjoy the routine of life. I seriously have not dated for the past three years because I wanted God to bring the right person my way. I didn't need to date back and forth because I knew he would bring you if I was patient."

Penelope's heart melted and she thought, Wow, he said, you. *God did show me the vision of Richard, and I can't keep thinking that he's going to be perfect. I'm not going to question God's judgment or put him in a box.*

They reached Penelope's house and, as always, when they all went out together the kids never wanted to leave each other, but tonight was a different story. They were tired enough to want to go to bed. Richard and Penelope kissed each other goodnight, passionately. Richard said, "I'm glad we had that talk, Penelope."

She smiled and said, "Me too. We'll talk more tomorrow."

Penelope tucked her two little bundles into bed. As she was heading to her bedroom, her inner spirit prompted her to remember two visions God had showed her seven years before. The first vision was during the tail end of her marriage. She saw herself and a little girl with long dark brown, curly hair with beautiful blue eyes. They were both dressed in white gowns, walking through a park located high on a cliff with a view of the ocean. She and this little girl walked near the edge of the cliff and looked out into the water. Out on the water was a big white cruise ship full of people having fun and living it up. The two of them knew when they looked out onto the ship that her husband was on that ship. Penelope wanted to jump down into the water and swim to the ship and pull her husband off of it. A voice from above said in a gentle but firm tone, *No! You can't do that, he's already made up his mind. Nothing you do will change that.* She and the little girl were crying and holding hands while standing at the edge of the cliff. The wind was blowing their hair back from their faces and their long white gowns were flowing in the breeze. Later, Penelope had figured out that the little girl was her daughter and that her husband was never going to change his ways. He wanted to have fun, not be a husband or a dad.

The second vision was also during the last days of her marriage. This vision showed her and her two children living somewhere else. The place was not familiar and they were living in a different home. In this house was a tall man wearing a baseball cap standing in the background. The feeling she gathered from the vision was that this man would be her future husband. The first time Penelope received this vision, she woke up startled at the thought that she would be with another man, especially since she was still married at the time. *How could this be? Am I thinking like this because I'm not happy? No, I know the difference between my daydreams and the visions God gives me.* God gave her the same vision again, and it showed her and the two children living outside of the state of Maryland in a different home. Again, it was the tall man wearing a baseball cap. She could not see his face in the vision and that drove her nuts. The point of the vision was to show her another man entering their lives who really cared about them and to show that he, too, loved the Lord.

Penelope and Richard had now been dating for about three months, since December. They both were feeling as if they had known each other much longer, which is something they had not felt with anyone else before. Almost like soul mates.

Richard arranged for his parents to meet Penelope and her two children by having lunch over at their home. They wanted to just hang out and get to know each other. All went well during the beginning of their visit; Richard's mom loved gardening and led Penelope outside and showed her all around their beautiful garden. She was able to name all her flowers and plants by the Hebrew names and explained how she and Richard's dad created their garden. As the two of them conversed, Richard came outside and stood behind his mother and began making funny faces, which made Penelope feel a bit awkward as she didn't want to laugh aloud and be rude while his mother was talking. Richard didn't seem to enjoy spending much time around his mother, but I found her quite interesting and brilliant. There is something about one's parents that we sometimes find irritating and this was true for Richard. It was quite funny to watch him act that way at his age. The three children were inside playing with toys that Richard and his siblings enjoyed when they were small.

After lunch, Richard's dad suggested that everyone take a walk to a nearby park. Everyone liked the idea enough to put their jackets on and head out the door. The kids were playing on the swings and running around. It was hard to talk to Richard's parents in depth because our kids are at the age at which they needed adults to keep a watchful eye on them. Penelope appreciated the distraction though; it eased the tension a bit. Richard's mom just talked away as she sat on the park bench, while Penelope pushed Cassandra on the swing. Richard was pushing Michael on the swing next to Cassandra. Richard and Penelope started staring at each other and Richard leaned over and goosed Penelope. Penelope then turned to push Cassandra but the swing had already swung back and hit Penelope right in the nose! She immediately bent over in pain. Her hands grasped her nose. It felt like it was broken. Richard lunged toward her and comforted her. Cassandra started crying because she thought it was her fault. Michael jumped off his swing to get Casey, but Casey was already running up a trail that was infested with poison ivy. He ignored the rope that indicated the trail was closed.

Richard's father had already left to pull the car up to the park and pick everyone up. As he got out of the car, he said, "What?! I leave for five minutes and all hell breaks loose! Is everyone okay?"

Richard and his mom were able to gather all the kids together. Cassandra stopped crying, Michael and Casey were retrieved from the trail before things got worse. Penelope sat up in the front with Richard's dad. His dad tapped Penelope's knee with his hand and said, "Don't worry; everything will be okay."

When they arrived back at Richard's parent's house, the kids settled down to play again. Occasionally, they'd go into the kitchen where their mom was sitting to check on her and give her a hug. Then they ran back into the living room to play again. Richard's dad pulled some Scotch out of the kitchen cabinet, filled the bottom of a glass, and gave it to Penelope. Finally the pain started to subside. Penelope was afraid her nose was broken, but it wasn't. Boy, was that close.

"What a way to meet everyone!" Penelope said. "I think I'm feeling better now."

Everyone started laughing. Richard's parents knew then that the two of them were going to be okay by the way they handled the situation. Also, judging by the way they were looking at each other, Richard's parents were smitten by Penelope and her kids.

The next day Richard came over to Penelope's house so they could head out on a long run together. They were training for a half-marathon down in the gorge, which is the most beautiful part of the Columbia River in Washington State. Penelope had been in triathlons and races in the past and had found that exercise not only gave her a clear mind but also made her feel good about life. Richard had done some running in the past and also loved softball, of course. They usually met at Penelope's house and then ran from there, having fun mapping out different routes.

"Ok Richard, are you ready?" Penelope asked. "We're going to run eight miles today, right?"

"I'm ready, babe!" Richard said.

They both headed down the street together.

"Man, the race is only about a month away."

Richard nodded. "Well, do you think we're running enough distance or are we going too far?"

"You always want to run your targeted distance at least once during preparation for your runs, and we've done that twice," she said.

Excited, Richard said, "Great! That means we're totally ready, right?"

"Oh yeeeaah, we've been strong in our runs and have been getting plenty of rest other than our lengthy phone calls into the wee hours of the morning."

Richard had a cute smile on his face. He was thinking this was becoming more and more difficult going back and forth from each other's homes. The kids were having a tough time saying goodbye when they got together. He said, "Life would be so much easier if we were all together under one roof, don't you think?" As butterflies went off in her stomach, Penelope said, "That does sound appealing."

Richard looked over at her and said, "Where did you get that jacket?"

Her jacket was a neon fluorescent yellow, bright as the sun.

"Oh, I bought this jacket at the running shop."

"Well, it looks like the ones that the club has. You didn't get that jacket from the club?"

"No, I just said 'it's from the running shop.'"

"Well, it reminds me of the jackets that you had to earn from the club for the 'Hood to Coast' event," he said.

"I know where you're going with this, but that's not where this jacket is from."

Richard had been a little disturbed at the recent discovery that Penelope had dated the same man that his ex-wife had interest in. His name was Earl, one of the owners of the local fitness club. The bright yellow jacket only reminded Richard of a certain group that hung out at the fitness club. Penelope tried to reassure him that there was nothing to worry about. She started to wish she'd never dated Earl. How was she supposed to know that his ex-wife was interested in Earl?

"Look Richard, Earl is not the committing type. Obviously the relationship with him would have never gone anywhere. I will say, though, every relationship you encounter has its purpose."

Richard interjected, "What kind of purpose was there with Earl?"

"I'll tell you, you take the positive from each relationship you're involved in and move forward with what you learned. I know your ex-wife hurt you and I wish I could say I never dated that guy for your sake. You are far better than him, so I'm not sure what your ex-wife saw in the guy."

"Are you saying you're glad you dated him?" said Richard.

"Yes, I am. There are things that I needed to learn after my divorce and, by dating Earl; it helped me know who I am and what I need in a relationship. In other words, in my heart I knew that relationship was never going to get serious. I needed to date people so when I met Mr. Right, I would know without a doubt that that man is the one. Then I would never think in the back of my mind that maybe somehow I missed an opportunity with someone who could be better for me. You, on the other hand, needed to stay out of the dating scene because you were hurt and you already knew what you want and need. I guess I should feel fortunate that you would even give me the time of day, huh?" She chuckled a little, but Richard didn't think any of this was funny. Richard was carrying a heavy heart. He just couldn't let the subject drop.

He said, "Well, I don't like the fact that you dated Earl, and I hate your jacket!"

Penelope's patience was dwindling now and she was really tired of talking about Earl, the jacket, and the people who used to go to the club. "Look here, Richard, I didn't even go to that club much and the 'Earl' thing has been over for years now and I happen to like my jacket!"

The two of them jogged in silence for a while and were just about at the entrance of the park now. Richard tried to keep up with her, but had a hard time because she was picking up the pace. There were two huge hills to run. Penelope ran up the first hill with ease, and then saw the second hill upon the horizon that was even steeper than the first. She was thinking to herself; let's see how he can prance up this hill. She heard Richard breathing heavily behind her. Her mind started racing like her body. *Unbelievable! This guy acts like I shouldn't have had a life before him. I'm thirty-six years old for crying out loud! Just because he decided not to date doesn't mean I should have.*

Richard shouted, "Wait up! I'm sorry for getting you upset!"

"No you're not," she shouted back. Richard finally caught up to Penelope and they finished their eight-mile course ten minutes faster than ever before! Breathing heavy, Richard said, "I'm really sorry Penelope, I just have a hard time knowing you were with Earl."

Both Richard and Penelope were out of breath. Penelope paused for a moment, and then said, "Richard, I wouldn't like it either if I knew someone you had dated before, but you can't keep holding onto that. You need to let it go so you and I can move forward."

"I will work on that," Richard said, "and I'm not saying you and I can't move forward."

"Then you need to ask God to help you to forgive and let go." She was thinking, this guy is going to need some time to heal.

They made it back to her house and guzzled some iced tea. Richard was concerned that Penelope was changing her mind about their relationship. She reassured him they just needed to continue to talk more about their feelings and not leave anything out. Most importantly, they needed to seek God and pray about what God wanted them to do.

Later that week, Penelope invited Richard and Michael over for dinner. She had planned a really special meal for everyone. They had marinated olives, ground turkey tacos, salad, Spanish rice, and ice cream for dessert. When Richard and Michael arrived, Michael handed Penelope a baby pull-up that was a sample mailer. His little face was smiling and Richard searched Penelope's face, wondering if she would be interested in having children with him. He asked her, "So what do you think about that pull-up?"

Penelope really was leaning toward the idea of not having any more children, but her heart was slowly melting around Richard. She just said, "Well, I'm not sure about that one yet, but I'm thinking about it a little."

Richard's face lit up with a smile.

Cassandra came up behind her mom and asked if she could have the pull-up. Her mom said, "Sure you can, sweetie" thinking that she probably would use it for one of her dolls. Cassandra ran up to her mom a few minutes later and said, "Guess what I have on?"

"What?" Her mom turned

"The pull-up mommy and I'm gonna see if it really works." Standing next to their refrigerator, she actually wet in the pull-up!

Penelope started laughing really hard and Cassandra just stood there smiling. Penelope told Cassandra to go change and wash up because it was time to eat. Everyone sat down together, talking and laughing. Richard and Penelope stared at each other and both knew they were thinking *this is good and it definitely feels right.*

The Ex's Meet

Casey and Cassandra's dad wanted them to visit him in Michigan for the weekend. He arranged to fly in and pick them up, and then he always flew back with them as well. This was the perfect time for Penelope to get to know Richard's son better. Penelope said,

"I'm really happy that I'm able to spend some time with you and Michael this weekend," said Penelope.

Richard nodded. "It's fun spending time with each child and discovering who they are. It's been a fun little journey. Now tomorrow at Michael's baseball practice will be the real test-- with his mom, Crystal. Also, don't forget that I'll be coaching so I won't be able to sit with you." Penelope could feel her stomach tighten up on that thought.

Penelope, Richard and Michael spent time playing games, having dinner together and reading books. Saturday afternoon came around fast, and it was time for Michael's baseball practice. The plan was for Richard and Michael to go to the field first, since they needed to arrive early. Penelope would then walk to the field a little later. She walked alone to the practice field. *I hope this isn't going to be awkward. I really wish Richard could sit with me.* As she neared the field she felt a little nervous, but confident that she would get through this. *Besides, how bad could it be? We already know each other from the athletic club, right?* She arrived at the field and glanced around to see if Michael's mom was there yet. Penelope felt funny just sitting there watching while Richard assisted with the team. The second Penelope glanced away from the baseball field; she saw Crystal walking toward the field with her white blonde hair pulled back in a ponytail and dark sunglasses on. Crystal walked right up to Penelope and sat down next to her and said, "Hi." It had been a long time since they'd spoken so she was surprised that she would sit right next to her. Penelope said Hi back.

Crystal started talking about the fitness club and some of the people that they both knew. She then asked Penelope if she still signs up for triathlon events. Penelope told her that she mainly does running now.

After about fifteen minutes of casual conversation, Crystal asked, "Who are you here for?" Is your son here? It's Casey, right?"

Penelope thought well here goes. She took a deep breath and answered, "Yes, my son's name is Casey, but he's not here. I'm actually here with, uh, Richard."

Crystal leaned back slightly for a second with a surprised look on her face and then said, "Ohhhhh, now I get it! Michael has been asking me all the time if we can go to Penelope's. All this time I thought he meant the Penelope's Peaches restaurant!"

Crystal started laughing but Penelope knew that it was not a pleasant laugh at all. Crystal then turned and said, "So he wanted to go over to your house all along, huh?"

"Yes, he's been over to my house on several occasions to play with Casey and

Cassandra. They all three really get along well."

Crystal suddenly went quiet, and remained that way during the rest of practice. Penelope couldn't blame her. Finally baseball practice was over and everyone went home.

Crystal left with a very quiet goodbye. After she walked away, Richard ran up to Penelope and said, "So how did it go? I can't believe you guys were actually talking!"

Penelope said, "Surprisingly enough, it wasn't that bad at all, but she definitely has the picture now. I'm not sure she likes it either."

They both grinned tentatively. Richard said, "Well, I don't really want to think about that right now; let's go home."

The three of them walked back to Richard's house to make dinner. As they were eating, Penelope reminded Richard that they had one more ex-spouse meeting tomorrow when Casey and Cassandra returned from Michigan.

Richard said, "Wow, this is the wonderful 'meet the ex's weekend' isn't it?"

Chuckling, Penelope said, "We knew it would come down to this sooner or later, so let's just get it over with." They both gave each other a hug, and Penelope was thinking *this is too good to be true*.

Sunday arrived and it was time for Richard to meet Casey and Cassandra's dad, Tony. Tony and his wife, Liz, dropped the kids off at Penelope's house. They all congregated in the kitchen and ended up talking for a while. Penelope noticed how Tony was eyeing Richard, and Liz was watching how Richard looked at Penelope. Penelope was never concerned about how the four of them would get along because there never really was a lot of tension between Tony and her when it came to the kids. They may have not agreed on everything, but they usually were able to be cordial toward one another. It was time for Tony and Liz to leave, so they were very pleasant and said their goodbyes. Casey and Cassandra were excited to see their mom, Richard and Michael.

Richard said, "Wow! That went very well."

"Oh, I wasn't worried about them like I was with Crystal," said Penelope and they both laughed. The rest of the day was spent with all of the children and dinner at Penelope's house.

Later in the week, Penelope had a long, hard day at work and all she wanted to do was come home and snuggle up with the kids. They arrived home and Penelope tried to think of what to make for dinner. "Hmmmm, we could have spaghetti, noooo. Ohhh, how about mac-n-cheese? The kids would love that!"

No mom, we're tired of that too."

"Got it! We'll grill burgers tonight. It's such a nice night, let's have a cookout!" So they pulled their tiny little charcoal grill out from underneath the deck and lit the fire. While waiting for the grill to heat up, Penelope started making salad and other fixings for dinner. Casey was playing with his cars and Cassandra was watching her mom fix dinner. Cassandra kept following her in and out of the house and out onto the deck. Finally, Cassandra pulled on her mom's shorts to stop her and said, "Mommy, God is telling me something in my heart, something special."

Her mom kneeled down and said, "What is it?"

"God is really, really telling me to tell you, oh wow! Mommy this is really cool! God is telling me that you and Richard are to get married and he's the right one for you. He'll make a good husband for you and will be a really good daddy for all of us." Her daughter took a wisp of her mom's hair and tucked it behind her ear. "Oh mommy, you'll be so happy."

Penelope was amazed that her little six-year-old was being spoken to in such a loving way. *God, you are utterly amazing how you use my children all the time to answer my questions and concerns. I love you for this!* She looked down at Cassandra and gave her a hug and a big kiss on her cheek. Cradling Cassandra's little face with her hand, she said, "Good job for listening and thank you for telling me. Always remember to listen to God when he speaks to you."

Cassandra shook her head and whispered, "I will, mommy."

Marriage

It was time for another long run together since the Half Marathon at the Gorge was coming up pretty soon. Richard had been traveling a lot lately which made it a bit challenging to run together. Penelope and Richard had planned to run on a Thursday afternoon after they both got home from work. The plan was to run along one of their favorite trails, which is right alongside of Lilly Lake.

Richard picked Penelope up right on time and their babysitter, Kelsey, was watching all of the kids at Penelope's house. The kids were anxious for them to return from their run because they were all going to eat dinner together that night. She looked over at Richard. *He still has something else on his mind. I wonder what it is.*

They arrived at the lake and prepared to start their run. Richard said, "You know, I don't feel too well. Not sure how far I can run today."

Penelope said, "Ohhhh, that's what's bothering you! Don't worry about it; if we only go four miles, that's fine."

She sensed that maybe they wouldn't even get that far. Richard was very quiet. They started off on the run, anyway, and were on the trail about two miles. Near the two mile marker is a cute little pier on the lake. At that point Richard said, "You know what? I'm not feeling well. I think I'm going to throw-up."

She stopped immediately, placed her hand on his shoulder and looked him in the face. "Are you going to be okay?"

Richard slowly pulled her toward him, slid a diamond ring off of his little finger, folded both of her hands into his and said, "Penelope, will you spend the rest of your life with me because I want to spend the rest of my life with you."

She felt like she was in a dream, and her eyes started to puddle. She looked into his eyes, saw the twinkle of love he had for her, and said, "Yes, yes I would love to."

He then wrapped his arms around her and they kissed. They turned around to walk back to their car.

Richard said, "I was trying to so hard to make it perfect. I hope you like how I asked you. First I planned on asking you right after we crossed the finish line when we run in the half, but then I thought, no, I want her to have this ring on while we run together."

They held hands until they reached their car. When they arrived at Penelope's house, all three children ran up to them smiling, giving them hugs. Penelope then showed them her ring and announced their engagement. They were so excited, they started jumping up and down.

Cassandra looked at the ring and said, "Wow, it's beautiful, mommy! I told you that God wanted you two to marry!" Casey gave his mom a big hug.

After making announcements to family members and parents, it was time to plan their wedding and bring two homes together under one roof. Of course, this was not going to be easy, but it's the kind of work that is worth it in the end. Initially they were dreaming of a Christmas wedding but after assessing their situation with the children and themselves, they decided it would benefit everyone to have their ceremony in the summer. Their wedding would have to be orchestrated within a four-month period now instead of eight months. They believed if they worked together, they would be able to do anything.

The plan was to put together a wedding, sell both of their existing homes and purchase a new home for their family within that four-month period.

Richard said, "First thing we need to check is that Pastor Frank is available to perform the wedding ceremony."

Penelope made the call and discovered it was a good thing she had; he only had one weekend available in August so it was perfect. After all, Pastor Frank had been part of the plan that brought these two together. During their conversation, Pastor Frank did suggest it would be a good idea to take a "marriage test." At first, Penelope was a little hesitant, but then decided it would be a good idea since things were moving fast and they would have responsibility for the "All American" family. They both met with Pastor Frank at a later date and were instructed not to discuss their answers, as that would not benefit the outcome of their testing. They were able to take their test at home and then come back and meet with Pastor Frank to discuss the results. So that's what they did. The test was a great idea because it covered all topics in a relationship: family values, finances, future goals, children, where you see yourself when you retire, etc.… Pastor Frank informed them that some couples who *really* thought they were meant to be together had discovered that they were not on the same page at all. While others discovered that they were more compatible than they thought.

It was time to meet with Pastor Frank to discuss their answers. Penelope was a little nervous but confident because she knew that God had brought the two of them together. Richard was also a bit nervous but he also knew they were meant to be. Pastor Frank said, "Before we go over any of your questions, I need to ask you two something. Did you discuss your answers or go over the test together at all?"

They both said no, as they glanced over at each other. Penelope fidgeted. *Wow! I hope he doesn't think we cheated, especially for something this important.* But she also thought maybe some couples would want to be together so desperately, they would fudge their answers. *Not this girl,* she thought to herself. They both explained to Pastor Frank that they in fact took their tests separately but then called each other and discussed their answers afterwards. No changes were made after taking the test.

Pastor Frank said, "Okay, I believe you. I just had to ask because we have *never* had any answers come back as close as yours have. All of your answers matched almost perfectly. So, the only concern I would have then is that there may not be enough room for disagreements. Disagreements can be a good thing for relationships, but I do feel in your case that it's not going to be a problem. A question for you, Penelope. Do you realize what you're getting yourself into?"

Pastor Frank looked over at Richard and said, "Have you told her?" Richard looked at Penelope and Penelope said, "Yes I do, but is there something else?"

Pastor Frank said, "I don't mean with Richard. I mean with his ex-wife." Richard looked at Penelope and said, "She is aware of her."

Pastor Frank said, "Ok, because it's going to be a challenge with her around." Slightly bewildered, Penelope did not know exactly what he was referring to other than your typical ex-wife getting jealous or having issues with Richard moving on with his life. She had felt everything was okay. Suddenly she wondered because she felt Pastor Frank knew something more.

After their meeting, they decided to go sit and talk in a restaurant. Penelope said, "Okay, what exactly is Pastor Frank talking about?"

"He's talking about how Crystal can be very difficult if she doesn't get her way," Richard said, "but you don't need to worry about it."

"Well, it seems like I should. Should I worry about how this will affect our kids with someone like that?"

He looked into her eyes and said, "If God wants us together then he will give us the strength to deal with it. Trust me, she cannot break what we have. Everything she tries to dish out will be nothing compared to what we have together as a family and what God will provide for us and the kids."

All of sudden, Penelope had peace and she put her worries to rest. Simultaneously, she realized, that just because God was bringing them together did not mean things would always be peachy keen either. She said to Richard, "I feel a lot better now, thanks."

They both were working full-time and had placed both of their existing homes on the market to sell. They worked on everything together for the wedding, from a place to provide flowers to the best location for their reception. On location, they decided on Lily Meadows Golf Club, which offered a large enough space for guests, dancing, not to mention their reputation for scrumptious food. The wedding cake was ordered through a renowned baker who worked at a local grocery store. His cakes and cookies were fabulous!

All was exciting during those moments of creating wedding plans. There were many nights when all five of them were out together. At the end of the evening the children wanted to spend the night, so it would end the way it started--everyone together. Those evenings of goodbyes always lasted for a long time.

Now it was time to search for a home together. They looked for weeks, and could not find a home that was large enough for Richard's business, three children, plus the fact that they both definitely wanted a child together (Richard managed to melt Penelope's heart in that direction). After many searches, they finally discovered a very nice home that would hold everyone, with an additional bedroom downstairs for Richard's office. Penelope didn't like feeling rushed by placing an immediate offer, and really wanted to look further, but time was not on their side. Richard assured her that they needed to do this so they could focus on their wedding, schools for the children, and their future. She agreed and they placed the offer. The house was theirs within two weeks, which left one month remaining prior to their wedding, August 24th of 2002. Richard's house sold right after the contract was put down on their new home. Penelope's house was still on the market.

The four weeks prior to their wedding flew by and before they both knew it, August 24th arrived! The day of their wedding, Richard, Michael and Casey were getting ready at the new house while Cassandra and cousins were getting ready at Penelope's brother's house. After Penelope had her hair styled at the salon, she went back to their new house to finish getting ready while the photographer took pictures of the boys. The old tradition of the bride and groom not seeing each other was a little difficult in their situation but understandable.

Family, friends and cousins all met at a nearby park for pictures prior to the ceremony. The weather couldn't have been more perfect. It was about 80 degrees outdoors with a nice breeze. This weather could be hard to come by in the Pacific Northwest. Lots of great pictures were taken of both sides of their families. After about an hour, it was time to go to the church for the ceremony. All three children were handsome and beautiful! The boys had black tuxes and the girls had purple dresses with a daisy atop their white sandals. Richard had chosen his dad for his best man and Penelope had chosen her sister-in-law, Marsha.

Richard and Penelope put together a CD program with various pictures of the two of them and their children accompanied by Pachelbel's Canon in D major. The congregation was watching the CD prior to the ceremony. Everything flowed together with the pictures of Richard and Penelope as small children and how they emerged into adults. It couldn't have been more perfect! There were pictures of them dating and pictures with their children. It presented the full package of how their family fell in love together. Their three children acted like they were siblings already. They were very happy that day. The two boys were especially happy, as Richard's dad kept slipping them some M&M's to keep them still during the ceremony.

The reception turned out beautifully with family, friends and cousins all engaged in conversation, as well as time out on the dance floor. The children danced all night. Everyone had a fantastic time and now it was time for the two newlyweds to go off on their honeymoon to Whistler, Canada for four days! After they said their goodbyes at the reception, it was time to round up their children and get them off to their cousin's home. Penelope's parents, Casey, Cassandra and Michael were sitting in the limousine that would take them to her brother's house. As the newlyweds were saying goodbye and giving hugs and kisses to everyone, Michael starting crying and got himself so upset, he threw up in the driveway right outside the car. Penelope's dad started laughing out of irony and told them not to worry, they'd handle it. Cassandra started crying and said she wanted her mommy. Casey was so happy to be with his grandfather and other family members; he couldn't understand why the other two were upset. Casey just waved goodbye and blew a kiss to his mom. They drove off and Richard and his wife went back to their new house, opened up a few gifts, and then went right to bed in exhaustion. The next morning they were off on their fun-filled trip together.

During their honeymoon, they were enjoying every minute possible, flying in a helicopter over the Canadian mountains, bike riding, hiking, running, swimming, spa treatments and eating out in the most unique restaurants. They both knew they had their work cut out for them upon returning because they would be unifying two families into one, but with God, nothing is too big to handle.

First Year

Richard and his son had already moved into the new house gradually prior to the wedding and then, of course, right afterward, the rest of the family moved in. There are a lot of complexities involved with blended families, lots of changes to adjust to. All three children were adapting to a new parent, new home, new marriage, plus Richard traveled for his job and Penelope was still working full-time. After a month of their new lives together, both decided it would be a great idea for Penelope to stay at home as a full-time mother. She was very excited about that because it gave her so much more quality time for their family. God had blessed their family in allowing her to be home for the children, also providing extra time for Richard and Penelope to develop a stronger relationship. After being single parents for such a long time, it took some adjustment, but was well worth it!

In addition to all of this, Richard's ex-wife couldn't stand the fact that Richard was moving forward with his life, and she didn't want another mom involved with her son. She started by asking for more child support, along with a modification of the parent plan. Pastor Frank's warning was starting to make sense to Penelope now. This woman did not know the meaning of "logic." Anytime basic issues were discussed, Richard always wound up in an argument with her either over the phone, which lasted ten seconds, or through email. There was a constant email war. Even though there were going to be challenges with his ex-wife, there was wonderful news on the way. After two months of marriage, they were expecting a new baby!

Penelope was trying to find the perfect time to tell Richard the good news, but it was hard because they were so busy with their children and his job. Finally, Richard sat down for a minute and Penelope said, "Hey, do you remember when you said to me, do you really want a child together?"

He answered with a curious expression. "Yes."

She said, "With everything going on I hope you haven't changed your mind."

"I definitely have not changed my mind," he said. "I still want that very much with you."

Her face gleamed with joy. "Good, because we are expecting!"

Richard was in shock; he couldn't believe it had happened so soon. He also needed to go to an appointment but didn't want to leave. They hugged each other and then Richard left for his appointment, very happy about their good news.

Later that afternoon, Casey, Cassandra, and Michael were playing outside in the yard since it was such a beautiful day. Casey came running inside calling, "Mommy, Mommy, you need to come outside and see the dead bird!"

"What?"

There's a dead bird outside?"

"Show me where, Casey." So she ran outside with Casey, and Cassandra and Michael were in the backyard looking down at the dead bird on the grass.

Cassandra said, "Mommy, can we bury the bird in the ground? Poor bird, look at him, mommy."

Mom said, "I wonder why it's lying here in the yard. Maybe he ran into one of our windows. You guys can bury him if you want but *do not touch* him at all. He has bird germs. I'll go get the garden shovel for you so you can scoop him up and dig a hole. How does that sound?"

They all three shook their head in approval. Mom came back with the shovel, and Casey started digging a hole for the bird while Cassandra made him a nametag to go over the burial site. Michael sat and watched.

As time went on, the children continued to get along well, but it was difficult for Michael to go back and forth. Richard and Penelope were hoping that they could have Michael full-time because Michael's mom showed no interest of following the parenting plan prior to the marriage. But of course, after the wedding the parenting plan would be followed to a tee. This was the most discombobulated plan ever. Michael was expected to go between both homes three days on and then four days off every week! The days that his mom had Michael, she would pack a check-list that consisted of the number of Michael's socks and underwear that were brought over which she would expect to be returned the following week. Any kind of cold or allergy medications would be accompanied by a long note explaining in detail how to give doses, as if Penelope had never been a mother before. When you have God in your life, he will give you the strength to deal with any challenges. Crystal needed to go through changes regarding the marriage as well. Part of her behavior and antics were because she didn't want her son to have another mother. She was acting just like a mother bear. Is there a bear worse than a grizzly?

It was time to pick up Casey and Cassandra from school and as Penelope was walking toward the front entrance, she noticed

Michael and his mom leaving to go home. Michael's face lit up when he saw her and he gasped and said, "Look mom! There's Penelope!"

He was going to say hi to her, but his mom pulled on his shoulder, leaned down to him and whispered in his ear. As they passed one another, Crystal glared at Penelope with daggers in her eyes while she held onto Michael's shoulder tightly. All Michael could do was look down at the ground. Penelope thought, *how horrible for her to act that way. She should be glad that he likes his stepmother.* Penelope laughed nervously, and said to his mom, "Aren't you intimidating."

Fall had arrived. Richard's 20th high school reunion was scheduled in October, and located in southern California where he grew up. Richard really wanted Penelope to go with him. It sounded like it would be fun to discover the town where he grew up and meet people from school, but Penelope kept hearing that "inner small voice" telling her not to go. She really felt the urgency of needing to stay home with the children. She'd learned a long time ago to listen to that voice. Even if it didn't seem to make sense at all, there was always a very good reason for the built-in intuition that God gave each and every one of us. So the time came for Richard to go have fun while Penelope held the fort down. One thing that really made her feel good about Richard was that he always called her several times a day to check-in and make sure everyone was okay. Richard would only be gone for two nights, so it should be no biggie. He definitely married the right girl, because she was so used to being on her own, that Richard's travels did not bother her at all. Friday morning was the first day of holding down the fort, and the kids were off to school. Penelope was looking forward to meeting Richard's mom downtown for coffee and shopping. She was in the car on her way to meet his mom when she had a sudden feeling that something was going to happen. She felt she should stay home. Now what? She said out loud, "I just need some down time to have fun for crying out loud!"

This time she did not listen to that inner voice and she continued to head downtown. She cut her trip a little short and headed home after having a good time with Richard's mom. She walked through the doorway, and noticed a message on their answering machine. It was the school! They left a message stating that Michael had been pushed off the play structure and to please call them right away.

She immediately drove to the school and was told that his aunt picked him up and took him to the hospital. Picking up Casey and Cassandra, she drove to the hospital to see if Michael was okay. Upon arriving at the Emergency Room, they looked around the room for Michael's aunt. She was nowhere to be found, but they did see Jane, a friend of Michael's mom. Penelope was somewhat relieved because she knew Jane from the club and taught her two daughters in a fashion class. She and her children sat down next to Jane and patiently waited to hear about Michael.

Jane asked, "How are things?"

Penelope said, "Good, they're really good."

Jane asked again, "Are things really ok with you and Richard?"

Confused and taken aback a little by her comment, Penelope told her that they couldn't be better and that their family was getting along really well. The doors of the Emergency Room opened, and there was Michael, walking through with a sling around his arm, his aunt by his side. He smiled when he saw Penelope, Cassandra and Casey. Penelope stood up and walked over to Michael and asked how he was feeling. The aunt kind of kept her arm around his shoulder like she wasn't going to let them speak with him or touch him. Michael just stood there and his face went slowly from a smile to a frown. Penelope asked his aunt where Michael's mom was and his aunt replied hesitantly, "Well, she's on her way."

Penelope said, "She's out of town, isn't she?"

His aunt replied in a curt tone, "Crystal wants Michael to go home with me until she returns."

"Then she can pick him up at our house," said Penelope, "since this is our week to have him."

She said, "No, Crystal specifically stated that she wants Michael to come with me and not you!"

Suddenly, Penelope had a sick feeling in her stomach, not really knowing what rights she had as a stepparent and longing for Richard to be home. Penelope got her nerve up and said, "No, he's coming home with us."

Michael's aunt totally ignored Penelope, waved to Jane to come on, and started to leave the hospital with her arm tightly around Michael so he couldn't turn or look at us. Penelope tried to see his face and he seemed to be okay with his aunt; he wasn't fighting her. She knew his aunt wasn't a stranger to him, which made her feel a little more at ease.

As Penelope walked back to her car with Casey and Cassandra, the two were asking questions about Michael, "Is he going to be okay, mommy?" "Why isn't Michael with us?" "We want Michael in our car!"

Penelope was still looking over at the three: Michael, his aunt and Jane. She noticed Jane was walking a little ways behind them as if she didn't want to be seen and was too embarrassed to even look at Penelope. She was so mad at herself for not staying at home so the outcome could have been what God wanted it to be.

"Dang it!" she shouted, "I would have been home to receive that call!" The feeling of helplessness overcame her. Casey and Cassandra were crying in the car because they wanted Michael home so they could make sure he was okay. Penelope was so mad that Casey and Cassandra were subjected to that type of behavior and that they had their brother pulled away from them so rudely. Upon arriving home, Penelope immediately called Richard and filled him in. Richard was livid and wished he could be there to assist Penelope but he couldn't leave and what good would it do, anyway?

Richard and Penelope were grateful that Michael's aunt was available to pick him up, but she should not have intervened in that way at all. Once everyone was settled in at home, Penelope decided to call Michael's aunt. When she answered, Penelope told her she didn't appreciate how she handled the incident and that she was wrong. Penelope had to get it off her chest even though she knew it wouldn't get her anywhere. She had a righteous anger toward the aunt and Crystal. During the phone call, Michael's aunt was telling Penelope, "Michael said he sleeps on the floor and that you make him call you mom."

She said, "What? I don't make him call me anything. Michael always calls me Penelope, and why would we make him sleep on the floor? You're out of line! You know you should have let Michael come back over here!"

His aunt got quiet and then proceeded to say in a country accent, "Michael is my blood," and then she hung up on Penelope. Penelope could not believe what she was hearing! Where in the world did they come up with this stuff about Michael having to sleep on the floor? After she calmed herself down, she tucked Casey and Cassandra in bed.

After everyone had fallen asleep, she decided to go into Richard's office to check on the fax machine as it runs out of paper sometimes. Everything was fine, so she sat down at Richard's desk and started playing around on his computer for fun. Out of the corner of her eye, she saw something dark flash by her really fast. It was a swish of a tall, dark floating figure. Immediately, her hair stood up on her neck and arms. An eerie feeling hovered over her body, which gave her chills. As she glanced around the room, she didn't see anything. She said a quick prayer to herself, knowing it was not her imagination, although she'd hoped it was. After praying, it felt as if something was watching her from the corner of the office. She got up from the desk and left the room briskly. When Richard returned from his trip, Penelope never really thought to mention anything to him about the dark figure in his office.

During the first six months of their marriage, they followed the parenting plan for Michael, which was three days on, four days off. Michael had a difficult time adjusting to this routine because it was sporadic. Michael was constantly badgered by his mother with questions of what kind of activities were going on in the home and how he addressed Penelope. After the first six months of arguments between Richard and Crystal that always began with emails or phone calls, they realized that a change needed to take place within the parenting plan. There was an Option B on the Parenting Plan, which instructed that Michael stay one week on, one week off at each parent's home. This arrangement was a lot better than before; but, of course, there had to be a court date to implement it.

After a few months of badgering emails and phone calls, God used Penelope to steer Richard in the direction of closing the "power" door on his ex-wife by not answering her emails anymore.

Once Richard realized the outcome of not answering her emails, things grew a lot more peaceful and they only contacted Crystal when necessary.

Their family continued to prepare for the new baby. They were discussing whether or not to find out the gender. After many talks with the children, they decided to find out. The idea would work well, because they could plan their household accordingly. By this point, their pregnancy was well advanced. Their doctor recommended a genealogy testing since Penelope was considered to be a "high risk" pregnancy at the age of 36. After taking the ultrasound, doctors stated that their baby boy had a very strong healthy heart and was physically normal. All three kids participated in picking out a name prior to the birth. Cassandra came up with the name, Tyler. After tossing around a few names, they all finally decided on Tyler. The name Tyler represented "tying" their family together. The two boys were excited to have a brother on the way, and their daughter was both excited and disappointed since she was hoping for a sister.

Penelope and Richard finished preparing for their new arrival by setting up the baby crib, chest of drawers, and Penelope painted his room with Safari animals, clouds and a palm tree. Everything was all set for this little guy.

Second Year

Cassandra and Casey were off again in Michigan with their father for a couple of weeks in the summer, which was the usual routine for them each year. Michael was with his mother for a few weeks in the summer too. It was a great time for Penelope to relax a little before the birth. Their baby was due on July 6th, one day before Casey's birthday.

On the day their baby was due, there were no signs of labor yet. Richard and Penelope decided to go for a walk in the afternoon down by the lake to kill some time. They walked hand in hand and a couple of people passing by asked, "When are you due?"

Richard replied, "Actually today is the day! We're kind of hoping this walk will speed things up a little bit."

Penelope thought, Wow, I must really look big, and she just laughed and said to Richard, "You know what's going to happen, don't you? Our baby is going to be born tomorrow and he and Casey will have the same birthday." The two of them finished their walk, went home, had a nice dinner, and then went peaceably to bed.

The next morning, July 7th arrived with sunshine and warmth. It was a nice hot summer this year. The first thing Penelope did when she woke up was go to the bathroom. Like most pregnant moms, she'd been going in the middle of the night for the past two months. This baby is sooo heavy, she thought. While in the bathroom, she had her showing! Immediately she thought, OK, no contractions. *I hope this delivery will be like Casey's, Please, God, let it be like Casey's.* Casey's delivery was fairly quick, before she even thought much about the pain. Her mother always told her each delivery is unique. Of course, her mom would know since she gave birth to seven beautiful children. She then called downstairs, "Richard! It's time to pack up and go to the hospital!"

She could hear Richard shuffling around and then he ran upstairs. "Are you okay?"

"Yes, I'm just not sure how much time we have, but we don't need to hurry because I haven't really started any contractions yet."

Richard said, "No, let's go ahead and go now. That way, if something happens, we'll be there."

Penelope took her time getting ready, while Richard grabbed their suitcases He planned on sleeping in the hospital with them that night. As they walked down the hallway, they stopped and looked into the baby's room one last time before it was filled with their bundle of joy.

They arrived at the maternity ward in the hospital, checked into their room by 9:00 a.m. and that's when the contractions began. From that point on the contractions grew and grew until Tyler was born at 6:00 p.m. Looking at his little face and holding him, they agreed that he really did fit the name: Tyler. Richard was extremely helpful and they both worked together as a team. No painkillers were used during the delivery at all. The nurses kept asking but Penelope said that she didn't want the baby asleep while he was being delivered. The nurses knew this wasn't her first baby so they left the new family member, mom, and dad alone for a little while. Tyler started nursing right away and was absolutely adorable.

Richard's family came to the hospital to visit, along with Penelope's mother and sister-in-law. Everyone was excited to see their new addition to the family. Some family members were checking the baby's ears to make sure he didn't have the elephant ears Richard had as a child. With relief, they realized Tyler's ears were a normal size. Then they checked his toes to see if he had the "Morton" toe that Penelope has, and he did! When the second toe is longer than the big toe, Richard's dad called it "Morton" toes. He says it means that you are talented and smart.

Penelope's mom visited from the East Coast and she stayed for two months, helping out with the baby and their household needs. It was great to have her there. All three children were very excited to meet their new brother when they returned from their visits for the summer. Each one of them took turns holding Tyler. Tyler was sleeping when they held him. At one point his eyes kind of rolled open and then closed as if he were saying, "Can you guys please be quiet?" Richard took Tyler's lips with his index finger and made them move so it appeared that Tyler was singing all by himself, "Something is in my shooooorrrrtts." Everyone laughed and then Penelope put Tyler up in his room for a nap.

Some friends came over to visit and brought food that was absolutely delicious. One of Penelope's friends noticed that her kitchen corner cabinet was repainted. "Wow, that cabinet looks great," said Denise. "How did you have the time to do that?"

"I finished it during Tyler's naptime," said Penelope.

Denise shook her head. "You know, you should really start your own business."

Excited, Penelope said, "Really? Thanks Denise! You just confirmed it, because I've been feeling that way for a while about this type of work. For years I've been giving people advice on décor, color analysis, interior decorating. It's time to get this going."

Her mom was standing nearby. "I can't believe she had the energy to get it all done with the baby, she said. "It looks great, you did a good job, hon."

"Thanks, mom. What should I call my business, maybe something fancy or a French name?"

Denise said, "No, just keep it simple, like Penelope's Designs or Designs by Penelope. "I love it, Denise! It's simple and to the point."

Denise said, "Designs by Penelope covers everything you would offer in your business."

Later on that day, Penelope ordered business cards and made flyers to give out to people. She was also able to connect with someone who worked for a mortgage company. They placed several articles in their newsletters about her business to, hopefully, generate some response. She didn't want to do too much with a new baby to care for---just keep it part-time until Tyler grew older. It would be perfect, she could work out of the house and stay close to the kids at the same time. Penelope thought, Thank you, God, for using Denise to help me out with this.

Richard had mentioned that he really wanted another child. Penelope responded, "Don't you know that you never ask your wife that until at least a year has gone by?" He kind of chuckled and said, "Yes, but you're so good at it and look what kind of babies we make."

She loved that he felt that way, but knew in her heart she could not handle any more kids. They came to the realization regarding why God brought all of them together and why one child made sense and not two. They had two McAllister's and two Andersons. What's funny is that both Richard and Penelope had mentioned this to their mothers even before they had Tyler. Both moms said they felt in their hearts that one child was best.

You never know what would happen down the road. Both women said they knew it was from God, and they felt led to tell the couple so they would have peace about it. They both finally did have peace about it and trusted in God.

Even though there was so much peace within the family; there was always the outside force of Richard's ex-wife trying to cause dissension. Once again, Richard came walking back from the mailbox with court papers in his hand. As he opened the door, you could feel the tension coming from his very pores!

Penelope said, "Now what?!"

Frustrated, he answered, "Looks like Crystal wants to modify the child support and schedule a deposition."

"What the heck? That girl cannot stand the fact that you have moved on with your life. Sheesh! You would think now that she's remarried, her life would be going well."

Richard replied with some relief in his voice, "Well, after reading this doc, it looks like we won't have to go to court this time. It would be just through the attorneys. There's another date set within another month to attend the deposition. Once again, I have to reschedule my business around her stupid court crap!"

The deposition came up quickly and Richard went by himself, since there wasn't any sense in Penelope attending with Tyler. Plus it was scheduled in the afternoon and she wanted to be home for the kids after school.

Richard arrived home from the deposition and said, "You would NOT believe the stuff that was brought up in the session today! Crystal was asking what we have Michael call you? How much money you've made in the past? What your profession was in the past? Where you used to live? Unbelievable! Half the stuff was inadmissible, but some of it I had to answer. So our attorney asked questions about Crystal's new husband, Steven. Of course they were questions that pertained to the case. So now that she is remarried, the child support will go down a considerable amount, which is in our favor. It was so funny, because Crystal brought her sister, and our attorney told her that she had to leave. Ha! She looked so stupid and insecure with all of her irrelevant questions. Our attorney finally said, 'Okay, how much longer do we need to put up with this nonsense?' I cannot stand her Penelope. She is such a pain in the butt!"

Penelope said, "Richard, don't worry we will get through this because we have God on our side."

Third Year

Penelope received another vision… This time she went to heaven and, when she got there, she was standing at a black iron rod gate that was both tall and wide. There was an angel in a white gown standing by just looking at her. She asked the angel if her dad was there and the angel pointed inside to where her dad was standing. It was beautiful in heaven! There were actual streets of gold just like the Bible talks about, and she saw her dad sweeping the streets with a golden broom. He was dressed in his favorite outfit, which was tan khakis, a red plaid shirt, and his black shoes. Her dad always likes to putz around doing things like sweeping and keeping up with the garden he and Penelope's mother managed together. In her vision, she said, "Hi dad! If you want, we could switch places? Do you want to?"

Her dad looked up at her and said, "No Penelope, I'm here aren't I? I made it, didn't I? Besides, the Master wouldn't have it."

"I love you, dad," she said. He said he loved her too.

The angel pointed up to the top of a huge mountain rock that had rugged edges, no trees, just a flat smooth face in blue and purple hues. Within the rock itself, there was a glowing blue light as if it were hollow within. The entire rock wasn't glowing, just a particular area. That glowing blue light was exactly where the angel was directing her to go. She didn't want to leave her dad, but the angel pointed in such a way that demanded immediate obedience. So she said, "Ok, I'm going," as she chuckled aloud. She then floated up to the spot where the blue light glowed and right at that moment is when she woke up from her vision. She started to cry because she knew that the vision meant her dad was going to die and go to heaven. It was a great thing he was going there, but was also sad because she and her family would miss him dearly.

She called her mom and described the vision.

Her mom said, "Penelope, I have to tell you there are some things going on with your dad and they're not good."

Slightly shocked, Penelope said, "What stuff is going on?"

Her mom explained, "Well, when he goes up and down the stairs he has to catch his breath, and then he breaks out in a cold sweat."

"Mom, it sounds like something is going on with his heart!"

Her mom sighed and said, "I know, but you know how stubborn your dad is. He won't go to the doctor. If something does happen, the most important thing of all is that he will be accepted into heaven. Don't worry, hon, I'm taking good care of your dad. Just keep praying for him." They hung up and Penelope said a quiet prayer to herself.

Penelope usually talked to her dad quite a bit anyway, but from that point on she began making more calls.

One time when she called, her dad asked her, "Why are you calling so much lately? Is everything okay?"

"Yes dad," she said, "I just miss you guys and I like talking to you."

He said, "When are you going to visit again?"

"Well, we were thinking of visiting for your fiftieth wedding anniversary."

Her dad then said something odd, "That's if I'm still here then."

Confused, she said, "What do you mean by that, dad?"

"Nothing, just maybe you should visit sooner is all."

"We will try if we can."

She knew her dad would never tell her what was wrong because he was just that way. Then he said, "I hope you enjoyed your life growing up and that we provided good things for you."

"Are you kidding?" she said. "We have great memories of the Magothy River trips. Many good times at Christmas, plus all the neat things we did with our neighbor friends. Gosh, we always had great food to eat, nice clothes and I can't think of a time when we went without. You should be proud of yourself, dad."

Her dad said, "I certainly hope so, daughter."

"Dad, you have no worries at all. Are you wondering what's going to happen to you? We all have things in our past that we are not proud of and if you ask God to forgive you, he will. I know you are going to heaven."

He said, "I think I will, daughter, and thank you."

"I love you so much, dad."

"I love you too, daughter."

"I'll call you soon," she said,

"Okay, talk to you then, bye."

Four months later... The kids were getting older and so cute! All of them were doing well in school. Tyler attended preschool and was in a big boy bed now. Penelope loved being home for everyone and always had snacks ready for them after school. Casey, Cassandra and Michael were going into third and fourth grades already. Tyler had turned two, and for some reason he had started having trouble getting to sleep at night. It seemed like almost every night he would wake up crying.

Another disturbing night came, which didn't make sense because he'd always slept well as a baby. Penelope was telling herself that she couldn't keep waking up in the night and still have enough energy for everyone else. What was going on? Penelope and Richard were getting very frustrated. It reached a point in which Richard would go in to check on him and sometimes have to actually spank him because he wouldn't go to sleep. The weird thing was that, almost every night, they were awakened at about the same time, 2:20 a.m. Outside, you could hear the train whistling as it passed through their small town. The whistle echoed up and down the hillside. The train whistle was more pleasant than hearing Tyler's cries. In Penelope's heart she knew the spanking was not the answer.

The next morning, Cassandra said, "Why did Daddio spank Tyler?"

Casey said, "Yeah, why is he doing that?"

"Well, we're having a hard time getting him to sleep, guys," said Mom. "Don't you worry, though. Richard is not spanking him hard. It may seem like it but, remember, he has thick diapers on."

Cassandra said, "Still mommy, I don't like it when he gets spanked."

"I don't either," said Casey. "Don't worry, guys, we'll figure something out. Your brother is in good hands."

"We need to pray about it, mommy," said Cassandra.

"You are absolutely right!" The three of them sat down together and prayed that God would help Tyler to sleep at night and that mommy and daddio would also get a good night's sleep. Daddio is the name that Casey gave Richard because he didn't want to call Richard by his first name. So, now, all three call Richard, Daddio.

Later that evening, Penelope received a phone call from her best friend, Meredith, who lives back East. She was so excited to hear from her. It had been a long time, but they had the kind of friendship that, no matter how often they talked, they could just pick up from where they left off. As they caught up on life, Meredith asked Penelope why she sounded so tired. Penelope explained that Tyler was not sleeping through the night and she couldn't understand why he kept waking up.

Meredith asked, "Did he always sleep like this?"

"No, he slept great as a baby and now, for some odd reason, he just keeps waking up. We've tried everything with him. He's not sick, not teething, it's kind of weird."

Meredith said, "Penelope, please don't take this the wrong way, but you guys live in an area where there's a lot of witchcraft. I'm wondering if it's not something spiritual."

"Oh my gosh!" said Penelope, "I should have thought of that! I guess with everything going on with our family and the court dates, I forgot about that sort of thing."

Meredith said, "You need to pray about it and ask God to show you what it is, because I can't shake the feeling that it's something along those lines."

They said their goodbyes and Penelope sat in bed thinking about what her dear friend had told her. She admitted to herself that she hadn't been thinking along the right lines spiritually and should have thought of that. She felt bad for Tyler. Richard stopped spanking him once she explained everything, and they both decided to handle things differently.

The next day Penelope decided to call her sister whom she had not spoken to in a while. She gave Leslie a call to see what was going on in her life. She and her sister chatted for a while, which was always enjoyable; they never ran out of things to talk about.

Her sister then asked, "How is your baby and everything?"

Penelope revealed Tyler's sleeping problem and said she wasn't sure of the cause.

Leslie prayed with her and at the end of their prayer, she said, "Uh-oh, Pen, this is not good. I feel like God is telling me that you guys really need to move and it needs to be sooner rather than later. Whatever it is in your house, its after Tyler and Richard. It kind of looks like a tornado and it's swarming around inside your house. They want Tyler really bad, and I'm not sure why, but God will direct you."

Penelope got goose bumps. "Well," she said, "I'm not sure how we are going to do that, but we'll trust in God to show us."

Leslie said, "Yes, God will show you, and I know it sounds premature, but the urgent feeling I'm receiving is really, really strong, Pen."

"Okay Leslie, we'll do what we can do. I think Richard wanted to get the church involved, too, to see if they will come to our house and pray over it."

"That would be good, but you still need to seek another place to go and get the heck out of there, Pen."

After they hung up, Penelope started to cry and she asked God, "Please, please Lord, help and protect us."

The next day, Richard gave the green light to hire a realtor and put the "For Sale" sign up. Penelope wanted someone who was a "shark" of a realtor so they could sell their home quickly. They finally found an agent who came over and went through the pricing with them. The realtor had mentioned that the asking price should be around $650,000. That sounded great because they'd paid $320,000 for the home. Wow! What an investment this would be! Flyers were printed, the "For Sale" sign was placed in the ground, and they started preparing their home for interested buyers.

Richard arrived home after several work appointments one afternoon and asked, "Hey, did you see that For Sale sign up next door?"

"No, I didn't, where is it, hon?"

"It's on the big lot next to us, right behind all of the fir trees. I guess the owner is selling that whole section, which is about twenty acres. You know what *that* means, don't you?"

Penelope said, "Well, it should be fine since it's on the other side, right?"

Richard replied, "It could. They may take down all of the forested area and then we're screwed for sure."

Penelope jumped in and said, "Ok, Richard, first of all you need to calm down a little and focus on the man upstairs. Maybe God will have it so it won't disrupt our yard at all."

"What's the second thing," he asked.

"Secondly, do you know how much I love you?"

His face settled and he gave her a hug. He said, "Let's get the church involved. We'll still keep the house on the market. Then if they can't help, we still have the other option in place. If they can, then we'll just take the house off the market and stay."

Penelope said, "Maybe we could list our house on the market in Hollywood, saying that we have ghosts in our house. We could have the 'Ghostbuster' directors stay for a night."

"Not a bad idea," said Richard, "but probably not what God had in mind." They both smiled and hugged each other.

The next day, a bulldozer pulled up onto the 20-acre lot located right next to their home! A builder had purchased the property and was preparing to construct thirty new homes on the site. The builder wanted to create the most beautiful gated community on Plum Hill. His plans didn't affect Richard and Penelope's home until they started taking down the 100-year-old trees that lined one side of their property. Penelope was watching through the window and became livid! She could not believe that the city would allow them to come in and rip up everything, leaving not even a small scattering of trees! She got on the phone right away and talked to the city planners and developers. They told her that there was really nothing she could do. Penelope informed them they were trying to sell their home and now they would be lucky if they received any showings at all. Who in their right mind would want to purchase a home with land next to it that looked like a bomb went off! Penelope hung up and called Richard right away.

"Richard, they are tearing down every single tree that lines our property. The kids have decided to protest. They made signs saying, "Keep Our Woods!" "No Building Allowed!"

Richard started laughing and said, "Wow, that's a good idea! Are they stopping and looking at you guys?"

"No, they're looking over to see who it is, but still working away."

"Well, I'll be home in about five minutes, anyway," said Richard, "so I'll see if I can't talk to the guy and find out what's going on."

"Richard, I spoke with the city already and they are not going to budge."

Richard made it home and walked over to where Penelope and the kids were. "Hey guys! Good job on the signs."

Michael said, "Hey dad, we're going to make them go away."

"Daddio," Cassandra said, "they're taking down all of the old trees and everything will be bare."

Casey looked upset. "Now we won't' have any woods to play in."

Tyler just looked up with his sign and grabbed hold of his dad's leg. Richard placed his arm around Penelope and said, "I'll go on over and see if I can talk to this guy and find out what their plan is."

He strode over to the man on the bulldozer. The worker saw him coming and turned his machine off and then jumped down onto the field to meet with Richard. Penelope and the kids were standing on the edge of the woods watching with anticipation. You couldn't hear what they were saying but there was some laughter. Richard headed back to where everyone was standing, and the worker started up his bulldozer again. As Richard approached his family, he said, "Well, it's not good. They're taking down all the trees that line our yard, and along the street behind their lot. Basically, they're going to build a bunch of houses on that property. They also will be checking the pins that outline our lot to make sure we are within our designated space. They are placing a public trail right next to our house, but the owner might be willing to plant some arborvitaes to give us some privacy."

Surprised, Penelope said, "What? I cannot believe this! It could be months before they're finished!"

Richard said, "I know, I would call the realtor and find out what we can do."

Penelope called the realtor and asked if they could do anything. The realtor said she would check to see if there are any building clauses violated when someone has a home up for sale immediately prior to an adjoining building project. She said she'd let them know.

The next morning it was time to take Tyler to preschool at Bright Futures. He was all set with his backpack and waterproof yellow jacket. He always looked so cute sitting in his car seat talking about his friends and his teacher at his school. Tyler's school was getting ready for their big annual fundraiser and this year's theme was "Cinco de Mayo." Penelope had painted a wooden shelf unit as one of the auction items. It was a peach/sage color stenciled with the words, Compassion, Love, Friends, Faith and Courage on the front and back of the shelves. She dropped the shelf off at the school in the morning while she walked Tyler into his class. That evening she and Richard planned to attend the auction to support Tyler's school. All the funds raised that evening would go to a brand new play area for the kids.

Richard and Penelope were excited because they knew some people at the event and it was nice to get out for the evening. Cassandra was over at her friend's house for a sleepover. A friend was watching Casey, Michael and Tyler. At the auction the Mexican food was very good, as prepared by a local chef, and there were tons of different baskets to place a silent bid on. At the end of the evening there was a surprise auction, a puppy dog! It was a yellow lab that was absolutely adorable. Everyone started placing bids of $100, $200. Richard leaned over to Penelope and gently put her bidding sign down. He whispered in her ear, "I thought you didn't like dogs? What are you doing?"

Penelope said, "I thought you and the kids wanted a dog?"

"Well, we do but are you sure you're ready for this? I think you've had one too many margaritas."

Penelope started to laugh and held her sign up again. At this point the bidding was at $400, and they won the puppy right then and there. Everyone was laughing and then Penelope's heart sank. Oh no, now we have two babies to take care of: Tyler and this dog. What was I thinking?! Then she thought, Okay we can do this, we can do this.... They both proudly walked off with the puppy in the little cardboard box and went home.

Upon arriving, their phone rang; it was Cassandra. "Mom, I want to come home."

Her mom said, "Is everything okay?"

Cassandra answered, "Yes, I just feel like I should come home-- like I'm supposed to."

"Okay, I'll come by and pick you up."

"You don't need to. Becca's dad will bring me over in just a few minutes."

"Okay hon, bye."

Becca's dad brought Cassandra back home and Penelope went upstairs to wake Casey and Michael and show them the new puppy. Everyone was so excited! The kids did not want to leave the puppy's side. Then the questions started, Can we sleep with the puppy? Can the puppy stay in our room? Is the puppy staying forever?

Becca's dad started laughing and said, "Oh, I remember those days; nothing like having a good dog around the house. Well, I better get back home, guys."

Richard walked him to the door and said, "Thanks for bringing Cassandra back, we'll talk to you guys later."

The next day they purchased all of the dog's supplies: a small crate, leash, bowl, food etc.... Since it was a puppy, Richard and Penelope decided to put the dog in their room; that way, she wouldn't go potty in the house. Puppy slept great the first night and didn't get up once all night. In fact, everyone slept great that night. The next day was a Saturday so everyone could sleep in, Yahoo!

All the kids wanted to do was to play with the puppy. Richard said, "What should we name this little guy?"

All the kids chirped in, "It's not a guy, daddio, it's a girl!"

"Okay, what should we name her?"

Everyone was going back and forth and then Richard came up with Maya. "Maya is perfect; we bought her at a "Cinco de Mayo" party."

"Maya is an adorable name," Penelope said. The kids agreed and they took Maya outside to play with her and get acquainted. Tyler woke up and finally met the new arrival. He loved her, but hated that she kept jumping on him and puppy biting.

The next evening, the kids were getting ready for bed early since they had school the next day. Penelope and Richard talked in bed for a while and then turned their lights out. In the middle of the night, Maya woke them up, growling. Penelope leaned over the edge of the bed and said, "Maya! Quiet!" Maya stopped for a second and then started growling again. Penelope watched her looking at a certain part of the room and then she started viciously growling like, whatever it was, was coming closer to her crate.

Richard said, "I wonder if she senses that there's something in our house?"

Penelope said, "She's definitely picking up on something.

He said, Sheesh! I cannot keep going on like this without my sleep. I'll be downstairs once again!"

Penelope said in a tired voice, "Sorry, hon. Thank goodness Tyler hasn't woken up, he just stirred a little in his bed."

The next morning, Penelope put the puppy in the garage so they could get their sleep. It seemed to work out better that way. She would bark when she needed to go out.

In the meantime, within the two weeks they had owned this dog, she had been a pain in the butt. She didn't listen about going potty and had peed on the carpet in the nice living room. She kept trying to bite the kids. Richard told Penelope that it was gentle puppy biting, but Penelope was convinced otherwise. One day when the kids were playing with Maya, Richard looked outside at the dog and noticed she really was trying to bite Cassandra. He immediately ran outside and pulled the dog away from Cassandra.

Richard came back in and said, "I really thought with your lack of experience with dogs that you were exaggerating about Maya."

Penelope said, "I told you that dog is not right—even the way she looks at me sometimes in defiance."

"What do you want to do?" said Richard.

"I think we should give her away, but only because there are way too many things going on and I do not have the patience for this right now."

Surprisingly, Richard agreed. Penelope called some of the teachers from Tyler's school and found someone who might be interested in their puppy. The next day, the gal came by and as soon as she walked up the driveway, Maya peed. Penelope handed Maya over to her, along with all of the dog supplies. The deal was to try her out for a night and see how it goes, no commitments yet.

The next morning, the gal called Penelope and said, "Your dog went bonkers last night. She jumped and nipped at my girls and would not listen at all. I'm going to have to give her back."

Penelope sighed and said, "Okay, I'll be here when you drop her off."

When the gal returned Maya, she told Penelope she called her mom and asked her if she wanted the puppy. "My mom said she would love another lab because she has had labs all of her life. You should expect a call from her soon."

So Penelope awaited the woman's call and was hoping and praying that she would call that day. She called the next day and came by to pick up Maya. Maya peed on the driveway again as the lady walked up the driveway. The lady asked, "Does she pee like that every time someone comes near her?"

Penelope laughed nervously, and said, "Yes she does, she did the same thing with your daughter when she came by."

The mom said, "Well, that's not good because it usually means they are intimidated and will act up."

Penelope said, "Well, if that changes your mind, we totally understand."

"No," the lady said, "I'll take her; she'll love her new home. We live on the water and we have another lab for her to play with."

Penelope said, "Oh great! Things should work out fine then."

The lady drove off and Penelope was so very thankful to see that puppy leave.

The next day their realtor called and shared with Penelope that the builder of the lot next door was not violating any building laws and that the best they could do is keep trying to sell, but bringing down the price would help if they were anxious to sell anytime soon.

After talking things over, they decided to lower the price to $599,000. Both Richard and Penelope came up with the idea to have flyers from the builder next door on display so when they had showings, the prospective buyers would have good information about the development. The value of their home probably would go up with a gated community right next door. The new buyer would also have the benefit of the community trail system that was being developed as well. The realtor loved the idea and got some packages together for their showings. They'd had about three showings so far, but with all of the construction in place, they were not sure how it would pan out.

The next evening Penelope and Richard went to the movies to spend some time alone. On their way home, Penelope's cell phone rang. She noticed it was her sister from back east. It had to be bad because it was midnight there. She answered her phone and her sister sounded really upset. She informed Penelope that their dad had suffered a heart attack and was in the hospital. She said, "I'm sorry Pen, but that's all I know right now. I wanted to let you guys know what has happened. And as soon as we find out more information, we will call you. Love you."

Penelope's heart sank! Memories flashed in her mind of her dad's conversation with her and she started to wish she could have lived closer. She started to cry. Richard held her hand and said, "Don't worry; your dad will be okay."

The next day Penelope's sister, Amber, called again and said, "It does not look good, Pen. Dr. Severs stated that he is 'skating on thin ice.' The heart attack caused so much damage that they cannot go in and perform surgery because dad's heart would not be able to handle it. He suggested that we contact all family members that don't live close by so you can come see him."

Feeling stunned, Penelope said, "I want to come, I just don't know how long I can stay."

Amber said, "When are you coming?"

"Well, I have to check and see when I can get a flight."

"Penelope, you need to leave and you need to leave now."

"Ok, I'll let you guys know when I'll be there."

They hung up and Penelope told Richard the news. Richard began searching airfare prices immediately. Penelope called her brother, Kevin, right away and asked what his plans were.

Kevin said, "I don't want to fly out if Dad's going to get better. Then in a couple of months we'll have to fly out again for a funeral."

"I'd rather see him alive, wouldn't you?" said Penelope. "Wouldn't you rather hold his hand and tell him you love him before it's too late?"

Kevin said, "I know you're right. I'm just having a hard time deciding because I have a lot going on right now."

"We could fly out together," she said. "Richard is booking a flight for me as we speak!" Kevin said he'd have to call her back.

Another day went by and Kevin finally called Penelope to tell her to go ahead and book his flight. Penelope was really excited they could go together. They'd leave the next morning and stay for three days to support the family. Her best friend, Meredith's brother arranged a hotel room for Penelope, Kevin, and their mother right by the hospital in Hershey, Pennsylvania. He had a time share and let them use it so they could easily walk back and forth from the hospital and help mom out with anything she needed.

The first day after their arrival, they drove up to the hospital to see Dad. It was really weird to see him lying in a hospital bed in the Intensive Care Unit, especially with an air tube down his throat. Their dad had already been in ICU for ten days prior to their arrival. Penelope walked over to the bed and took her dad's hand and held it in hers. "I love you, dad," she said. Kevin stepped over to the bed and said, "I don't know if you can hear us, dad, but we're here for you."

There was no response, but Penelope somehow knew he knew they were there. They stepped out of his room and headed down to the waiting area to meet up with the rest of their family. Pretty much everyone was there. Some of the nieces and nephews were even there. It was really good to see everyone and catch up on family news. Mom was stressed out and tired, but that was to be expected. Penelope and Kevin decided to take a walk outside and get some fresh air. The hospital was very nice with beautiful grounds.

Kevin said, "I don't mind telling you, Pen, this is really hard for me. I want to remember dad the way I knew him, not lying in a hospital bed. I think he would want us to remember him that way as well."

In a comforting tone, Penelope said, "Kevin, I know it's hard, but at least you have the opportunity to see him again and tell him that you love him. I think dad would want us to remember him when he was in a better condition as well, but he knows we're here and that means a lot to him."

Kevin said, "Do you really think he knows we're here?"

"Yes I do; it's one of those things I just sense."

The next day, Penelope, Kevin and their mom had breakfast together at Friendly's Restaurant. Mom filled them in on the procedures their dad experienced during the past week. There was some clotting in his legs and they placed a stent inside his thigh in hopes that this would keep the clotting to a minimum. Now they were just waiting to see if he was strong enough to be taken off the machines and breathe on his own. So it was another day of walking around, watching their dad, and going outside to talk and get some fresh air.

While they were all outside, Kevin received a phone call from his wife, Marsha, who informed him that their daughter's front tooth was knocked out during softball practice! Another player threw the ball when Jamie wasn't looking. She turned right as the ball reached her face. Marsha was able to locate her tooth on the ground and they took it with them to the Emergency Room at their dentist's office. They were preparing to surgically repair her tooth, hoping the roots would take and not die from nerve damage.

Kevin was upset that he wasn't there for her. Marsha did a great job taking care of things. After hanging up with his wife, Kevin just kind of sat there in disbelief. Mom told him not to worry and that Jamie would be okay. She also reminded him that she, too, had her front tooth knocked out in softball and now had a cap on her front teeth.

"Wow! I forgot about that," Kevin said. He somehow felt a little better after that reminder.

Later that evening, Penelope and Kevin went back into the hospital to visit their dad. At this point he was awake and had been trying to speak with the air tube in his throat. Their dad kept moving his hand around as if he was writing. After watching him for a few minutes, they realized that he wanted something to write with. He was trying to say that he wanted to go home. At that point, the doctors came in to check on him and make sure everything was working fine. The doctor then asked for everyone to meet with him outside of dad's room. Dr. Severs proceeded to explain that everything looked okay but that they shouldn't expect him to be able to do the things he could before.

"There has been a lot of damage to his heart that cannot be repaired," he said. "I'm just trying to prepare everyone."

He walked away and, after everyone digested that information, they went back into Dad's room. Dr. Severs walked into the room and checked on things again. Penelope looked at her dad and then glanced over at the doctor.

"Dr. Severs, will you please take out the air tube? I know my dad and he needs that out. If you don't take it out I'm not sure how long he can stay this way."

The doctor and Penelope locked eyes and just stared at each other for a few seconds with an unspoken understanding. Dr. Severs looked at their dad and seemed to be thinking to himself for a moment. You couldn't hear anything but the machines in the room humming along. He called in the head nurse and heart machine specialist to check his vitals and machines to see whether he was really capable of breathing on his own. Everything looked really good.

He then looked over at Penelope again, and said, "Okay, we'll take it out, and we will have everyone full staffed through the night to make sure he's alright." They pulled the air tube out of his throat and their dad let out a very loud cough and was hacking for five minutes or so. It took a few more minutes for him to gain composure because his throat was so very dry and raw. He finally became stable and everything was looking great. At this point, Penelope, Kevin and their mom were ready to go back to the room since it was very late, 11:00 p.m. They stood close to their dad's bed and he said in a scratchy voice, "Thank you. See you in the morning." The three of them left feeling relieved and more at peace since that was the first time they'd heard their dad speak since their arrival.

Next morning in the hotel room, mom received a call from the hospital stating that Dad slept through the night peacefully and he was awake and ready for visitors. Everyone hurried, got dressed, and walked over to the hospital. As they arrived, personnel were preparing to move their dad out of the ICU. He would now be in the regular wing of the hospital. It took awhile but they finally prepared his new room and settled him in. After being in ICU for ten days, you can imagine the type of back up a person would have from not going to the bathroom. Well, the nurses were trying to get him up to go to the bathroom by himself!

Once again, Penelope spoke up and said, "My dad has been in the ICU for ten days and you're expecting him to just get up and go to the bathroom! He'll fall and injure himself. Go get a bed pan!"

She then ran down the hall to the nursing station and informed the staff that they need to read their notes and to reassure her and their family that they will be monitoring him correctly. The nursing staff informed them that they would and they apologized to Penelope's mother. After all of that, everyone was ready to visit dad in his room. Dad's brother and his wife, four of his seven children, and mom were all there watching over him.

He opened up his eyes and when he saw Penelope and Kevin, he said, "Well, it must be pretty bad if Penelope and Kevin are here."

Everyone started laughing.

"You guys didn't have to do that…" he said, "fly all the way out here."

Penelope said, "Dad, of course we would come to see you!"

"Well, it costs a lot of money for you to travel", he said.

"Dad, we're not going to not come because of that. We love you."

Kevin added, "Dad, it wasn't a problem."

Dad smiled faintly. "Well, I'm glad everyone is here."

At that moment he was going through some memory lapses. He asked his brother questions about their childhood neighbors, along with memories of growing up.

He asked his brother, Jan, "Hey those neighbors…. They had a lot of money stashed away in their driveway didn't they?"

Jan looked into his brother's eyes with a bit of sorrow knowing that something wasn't quite right. Jan cleared his throat to answer, chuckled a little, and then said, "No, that was the joke, remember?"

Dad said, "But they really did have something hidden, right?"

Jan said, "C'mon you remember, that was the joke that they had put some money into a bag and placed it under their driveway, but we all knew it was a joke."

Dad said, "No, I know they had something in there."

Jan fixed his brother's hair and said, "That's ok, it's ok, Rod." Dad never liked his hair messy. The subject changed after that and they all made small chatter. Uncle Jan and his wife left the room for a bit and Kevin stepped out into the hallway of the hospital. Everyone else stayed in the room and you could tell they were wondering what would happen from here.

Unfortunately, Penelope and Kevin would have to leave the next day to get back to their families. It had been three days already, but they were very grateful to have been able to spend a little time with their other sisters and tell their dad how much they loved him before leaving. It was so very hard to leave that hospital room. Penelope held onto her dad's hand and touched his forehead gently and leaned over to kiss him. Kevin placed his hand on his dad's shoulder and said, "Dad, we'll miss you and we'll be thinking about you a lot. Sorry we have to go now."

Dad said, "I understand, you two need to get back to your families. Thanks for coming."

Outside in the hallway, the doctor informed the family that dad would have to go through therapy to regain his strength after being in the hospital for so long. He'd suffered some severe heart damage. He should be released within a week if everything looked good.

Dr. Severs said, "I do warn you, your father is skating on thin ice. The heart attack did a lot of damage and he may not live past another four months. He will be on quite a bit of medication and we'll have to monitor his condition." Everyone was surprised by the news, but very hopeful. Penelope told everyone to stay in touch and said to let them know if there was any way they could help. She and Kevin flew back home.

When Penelope arrived home, her family greeted her at the door with hugs and kisses. It was a very exhausting trip. It did feel good to be home again. That evening when everyone was in bed, Penelope and Richard were awakened by Tyler again. They could hear Tyler talking to someone! Tyler was saying in his little toddler voice, "No! You get out of ma room! These are ma covers!"

Penelope tapped Richard's leg with her foot and said, "I'll get him," and as fast as she could go, she ran into Tyler's room and picked him up. "What's wrong, pumpkin?"

Tyler held onto his mom and pointed to the wall and said, "Darr man, right there, mommy." She looked around and didn't see anything.

"Are you having a bad dream?"

"No mommy, dark man right there," as he pointed again.

"How about I sleep in here with you tonight?"

Tyler nodded his head and latched onto his mom. They snuggled up next to each other and tried to go to sleep. Tyler started to drift off immediately. Just as Penelope was dosing off to sleep, a dark shadow hovered over her and she felt coldness. She was afraid to look up, but did anyway, and when she did, she saw a dark outline of a figure that looked like a person but wasn't. The spirit's face was crumpled up in anger, wrinkled and ugly. It started to yell right in her face and said, "You're interfering, get out!"

Penelope sat up in Tyler's bed and spoke back to the spirit saying, "You get out in the name of Jesus! This is a house of the Lord and you do not belong here. I command you to leave right now in the name of Jesus! Our son belongs to God, not you!"

There was a cold chill in the room and she could tell that it did not want to listen to her. The darkness was so strong, she felt like it would consume her. Whatever it was, it was not going to leave. She got up, picked up Tyler and took him into her bedroom and they slept there the rest of the night. Richard went downstairs so he could go back to sleep.

The next day, Richard and Penelope prayed together. Penelope felt a righteous anger building up. She said, "I will fight this thing. It will not intimidate us."

Richard agreed. "Let's ask God what to do to continue to fight this. I thought they were supposed to leave when you pray the way you did?"

"Well, they are," she said, "I'm not sure why it's not." The thought of that spirit not leaving bothered Penelope. She called her mom for advice since she had experience in this field. Her mom said she needed to anoint their home with oil as an act of faith. They must believe that God would bless their home and protect them from evil.

As soon as they got off the phone, Penelope went into their kitchen and filled a little bowl with oil. She then took her finger and dipped it into the oil and made the cross symbol over each and every door and window of their home. As she did this she prayed to God and asked him to bless their home and protect them. Penelope immediately could feel that whatever was in their home did not like her doing this. She continued anyway and when she reached Tyler's room, she could feel the coldness; it gave her goose bumps. Her voice was a little shaky, but she came against the fear by prayer. She asked God to remove anything not of him and replace it with good through the Holy Spirit. Penelope could still feel the presence of darkness. She left Tyler's room and continued through the remainder of the upstairs of their home.

Later that evening, Richard and Penelope prayed together before they went to sleep; they did every night. Tyler had been sleeping in their room, which allowed him to sleep soundly all night. They pulled his mattress into their room on the floor next to their bed. In the middle of the night, Penelope and Richard's bed started to shake from underneath the mattress, which woke them both up.

Richard said, "Did you just feel that? Please tell me you felt that!"

In a slightly scared voice she said, "Yes, I did." They both were really wishing this was not happening. Penelope quickly leaned over to check on Tyler and he was sleeping just fine. She thought maybe it was Tyler kicking their bed, but he was not able to do that from where he was. Besides, he couldn't have shaken the bed that hard. So Richard and Penelope held hands and prayed together and this time Richard spoke out in prayer and asked for God's hand over their home and children. They both tried to go back to sleep. Once again, the bed shook and woke them up and this time it was harder. Penelope was really convinced this time it was *not* Tyler. She leaned over again and looked down at him and he was sound asleep. The force behind this shaking could not have come from him. The bouncing was from under their mattress. Richard said, "We have visitors again. Great! It's bad enough I can't sleep really well and now they're waking us up almost every night! I'm going to have to go downstairs."

"Oh no you don't!" Penelope exclaimed. "You are not leaving me up here alone, Richard."

Richard said, "Well, what am I supposed to do? You know once I'm up I have to go downstairs."

She was scared, but reminded herself of Christ's presence. With that, she rolled over to go to sleep. Later in the night,

Richard came back to bed. Penelope cuddled up next to him and he had goose bumps all over. She asked what was wrong. Richard explained while he was sleeping, he felt a cold presence around him and he had the feeling of not being able to move. It felt as if his body was being held down by some kind of force. He finally felt like he could get up from the couch and he ran upstairs.

She comforted him. "See you were supposed to be up here with us after all."

Richard said, "Well, I'm sorry. I'm just trying to get some sleep." They finally dropped off to sleep only a couple hours before dawn.

The next day Penelope called her mom again. When Mom asked how they were doing, she said, "Not good, mom."

"What's the matter, hon?"

"Well, where do I begin? We anointed the house like you suggested and I think it made it worse because they were shaking our bed last night and we prayed and told them to leave but they stayed and bothered us on and off through the whole night."

Surprised, her mom said, "Oh my! Well, why don't we pray together and see if we can't get any answers that way."

They both prayed and at the end of their prayer, her mom told her that God was revealing that there was something there that would not go away because some sort of ritual or act had been performed in their home. It had given Satan a "foothold."

"I don't know if the people before you were involved in some kind of satanic worship or witchcraft," said her mom, "but you need to find out what it is. And God is also saying that you need to leave as quickly as you can. Put on your armor and continue to pray for God's protection. I want you to look through your house and see if there is anything that isn't of God or maybe any markings that may be hidden on the walls or under the carpet.

Sometimes people get involved with things that are not of God and it provides a door for evil spirits to come into your home."

Penelope said, "Well, this house was only a year old when we bought it, mom. I don't think there is anything attached to it because of the age. You know how sometimes an old house can have a lot of bad energy or good energy over the years from people moving in and out?"

"Yes, yes I know what you mean hon, but this is not the case."

"Ok mom, I'll look around and see if I can find anything, but I really don't think anything was physically placed in the home."

Mom said, "Let me know if you need any more help."

"I will Mom, thanks." After hanging up with her mom, all of a sudden Penelope had a flashback of the inspection day before they moved in. The mother of the other family and her two boys were present at the house during inspection. Penelope also had her two children present with her. She could remember the mom looking stressed out and anxious to sell. At the time, she thought it was because inspections can make people nervous. Then another memory came to her mind. The youngest boy acted a bit strange. He had a pet snake in his room and they fed it mice. He pulled a frozen mouse out of the kitchen freezer, and Penelope thought he was going to show them how he feeds his snake. Instead, he started to play with the frozen mouse on the floor of the family room. He looked over at Penelope, Casey and Cassandra and kind of laughed in a sadistic way. Penelope was thinking she may have erroneously overlooked these facts. Maybe the mother really was anxious to leave because she knew there was something terribly wrong with the house! And perhaps, the spirits were after her son as well! She also wondered whether she and Richard should have prayed a lot more before they purchased the home. They rushed out in excitement over their new life together and forgot one of the most important rules of all, pray first!

Penelope was looking quickly through every upstairs nook and cranny. She looked through every single closet and examined the walls for any kind of symbolic signs or any trace of suspicious markings. She even pulled the carpet up from the floor in Tyler's bedroom thinking maybe they covered up some kind of marking underneath. Nothing was found. Then she remembered the attic above their bedroom, which was very difficult to get into. You had to get a ladder, remove a square piece in the ceiling of their closet, and then climb up the ladder and into the opening. Once up there, only a small area had floorboards. She used a flashlight and looked around as best she could, once again, with no signs of anything unusual. She then headed downstairs and looked through Richard's office, as well as the kitchen and dining room. The last spot to check was their crawl space. There was a pull-handled door located in the floor of their pantry. She pulled it up and out, and laid it on the floor next to her. She then climbed down onto the built-in-ladder that leads into the crawl space. Once down there, she pulled the string connected to the light and turned it on. With her flashlight, she looked all around down there, shining the light onto all of the wooden beams and insulation while looking in every corner possible. There were spider webs everywhere. Penelope prayed in her mind and asked God to show her anything that could be causing these weird spiritual happenings in their home. She thought, *I knew it, I knew there weren't any kind of markings like that,* but as she turned to climb back up the ladder, out of the corner of her eye, she saw a dark shadow sitting in the right corner of the crawl space. She stopped in her tracks, and did a second take over her shoulder. There was what appeared to be a witch in a raggedy black dress, boots, hat and long scraggly hair with a gray face masked by darkness. It was crouched down in the corner laughing just like you would hear in a movie, cackling saying, "I'm over here, Penelope, and there is nothing you can do. We're not leaving." Penelope could feel the evil and felt a cold rush over her entire body and she hurried out of that crawl space as fast as possible, skipping most of the rungs on the ladder, and just pulling herself up to the top. She then slammed the door down over the crawl space. Her heart was pounding and she felt relieved to get out of there. She thought, Okay, Lord, we're ready for battle until we can get the heck out of here. She then spoke out loud, "This family is protected by Jesus Christ and you have no authority over us. Father, pour out the Holy Spirit over us and send your guardian angels down upon this family to protect and guard us in the name of Jesus."

Penelope's mom had taught her a long time ago that God's Word states that anything not of him must leave you when you mention the name of Jesus. Anyone who is a follower of Christ has the authority to use Jesus' name (Philippians 2:9-11).

There were two different prayer groups at their church. One was the Intercessory Prayer Group, which specifically prayed for the church and people. The other group was the Bible Study Group, who had weekly sessions, which involved studying the Bible using different video presentations to gain strength from God's Word and its meanings. Penelope had attended the Intercessory Group at her church and thought of Pat, one of their prayer warriors.

She gave Pat a call. "Hi Pat, I need you to pray with me about something. We are having some spiritual issues within our home."

Pat asked, "What kind of spiritual issues?"

"Well, they started in Tyler's room bothering him at night and now they try to keep Richard and me up all night. I've seen a dark shadow in Tyler's room and in our bedroom. Of course we've moved Tyler into our room so he can sleep. They are also…"

Pat interjected, "You say 'they.' Does that mean you think there is more than one?"

"Yes, I guess…yes I do. A spirit has bothered Richard downstairs while he is sleeping while simultaneously a spirit has disturbed Tyler and me in an upstairs bedroom. And now, the other kids are being affected at night as well. Casey woke up the other night with a horrible dream. It was a dream about this house. In his dream, everything was colored gray and dark and gloomy both outside and inside of our home. He was trying to get our family together so we could leave. In his dream, there was a lake outside of our house and all the fish and birds were dead. Anything that touched our house would die and the only reason why we were okay was because God is watching over us.

Pat said, "Ok Penelope, I'm feeling like we need to pray and we need to pray right now."

Whenever Pat prayed for someone, there was always the sense of the Holy Spirit around. This woman had the ability to tap into God's presence and get answers. Penelope definitely felt protected just from talking with Pat over the phone. A few minutes after their prayer, God answered them through Pat. She said, "Ok, you are dealing with an evil straight from the pits of hell. There is nothing you can do to get rid of them because they have a foothold over that home. You need to get out of there as soon as you can because they are after your son and they are after your husband. Penelope, I believe you are strong enough to handle this. Stand firm and put on your armor every single day and keep asking for God's protection over you and your family and God will continue to keep your family safe, but you do need to move out of there immediately."

Feeling empowered and ready to start a mission, Penelope said, "Thank you, Pat. God just confirmed through you what my mom and sister have prayed as well."

"Well, Amen to that," said Pat. "I gotta go Penelope, but you do what God is telling us here, you hear me?"

"Yes Pat, we will move forward with this and I'll let Richard know right away. Thank you so much for taking the time out to pray with me."

"No problem, hon, we'll talk later, bye bye."

Penelope's heart was pounding and she had goose bumps all over. God confirmed exactly what her mom and sister had received through Pat. She now knew that this battle would not be won on these grounds like she had wanted to do. Penelope thought to herself, *Well, we need to make plans to get out of here now and now can't get here any sooner.*

While making dinner for the family that evening, Penelope asked Cassandra, "Can you get the French bread out of the freezer in the garage for Mom?"

"Okay, Mom, I'll be right back." Cassandra came racing back into the kitchen breathing heavy with the bread bag barely held by her fingers. "Mommy, I hate going into that garage by myself."

Her mom said, "Why? What's the matter?"

"Well, I always feel like something is watching me in there. When I went into the garage, I could feel something staring at me and then I heard something say, BOO!"

She gave Cassandra a hug and they held onto each other. Her mom said, "I'm sorry you got scared. Remember that God is always watching over you."

"Okay mom, I will." Penelope really started to get angry inside just thinking to herself how pathetic Satan is when his forces pick on little children.

Obviously it was time to get really serious about finding another home. Penelope and Richard started looking around for a home to purchase. This time they were going to pray and pray about it hard. They found a house that was absolutely beautiful and perfect for their family. Their realtor set up a time to view it and they loved it. It was close to Penelope's brother as well, which would make visiting one another easier. They went home to pray and think about it. The house was on five acres. The estate had a separate double carriage, and the house held four bedrooms, a playroom and a basement with a kitchen. It was priced rather high but allowed enough room for them to make a good deal. They scheduled a second visit, and this time they felt really good. Everyone was both excited and relieved. Richard placed their offer.

In the meantime, the main road to their existing home was closed because of a landslide that had occurred earlier that week. There was a lot of rain that spring and the mudslide had caused significant damage to some of the homes further down the road. Huge rocks, debris and mud had spilled out onto the road, blocking anyone from using it.

Three days later their offer was accepted with a contingency that Richard and Penelope be able to sell their home within a six-month period and the sellers be able to build on another piece of property they owned. Richard and Penelope thought, *Lord, here are the facts and we know you want us out of here. We pray right now that if it's your will, that our home will sell and we will be able move up to Snowy Mountain and get the heck out of here.*

The land next to their existing home was being built upon and was stripped of all trees and shrubs, and with all of the rain, it was one big muddy mess! Richard and Penelope had discovered through the grapevine that the land next door was not suitable to build upon. The land had too much run-off from all of the rain and the state would not allow it to be built upon until the builder covered up the entire twenty acres with plastic to keep the run-off from going down the hillside at the southern end of the property, thus stalling the project for another six months. Penelope informed their realtor of the issue at hand and she suggested dropping the price again and taking new pictures to entice buyers. The house would be listed as a "new Listing" again since the price would be changed. Their realtor came over to meet with Penelope and take new pictures. This time Penelope wanted to take pictures as well, just in case she could catch any spirits on her camera. Penelope had charged their camera in advance so it would be ready when the realtor arrived. The realtor came to the door and conveyed to Penelope she was really trying hard to help them out. Penelope couldn't help but feel like they were being defeated in view of the events taking place, but held onto the fact that God is in control. Their realtor set her camera and started to come up the stairs. Penelope was already standing at the top waiting for her. As her realtor approached, she said, "You know, I have sold quite a few homes and have the experience of sensing different vibes when you walk in someone's door. And, boy do some of the homes I have seen have some weird stuff going on."

Her realtor slowly ascended up the stairs, then added, "Oh honey, I have to say, what I'm feeling right now is not good. I don't know what to tell you."

Penelope said, "We have been having some issues and really need to sell it." The realtor made it to the top of the stairs and started to take her pictures for the flyers but her camera wouldn't work.

She said, "That's weird, I just charged it this morning because I knew I was coming over for this today. Let me try again." Her camera still did not work.

Penelope said, "Here, you can use mine, I just charged mine up today too." Penelope's camera did not work either. They both looked at each other with an unspoken thought. Something was definitely going on here.

The realtor said, "Well, I'll come back later to take these since nothing is working. And don't worry, we'll get this going. I'll be in touch, see you later."

Penelope followed the realtor downstairs to let her out. She then closed the door. As the door clicked shut she could sense a strong presence standing at the top of the stairs staring down at her. It was the same spirit that was in Tyler's room! Her back was still facing the stairs as she heard, "Get out! You're interfering!"

She then swiftly whirled around and said, "If you want us out then you better get someone in here to buy the house and *we* will leave!" She walked away, not caring if it had anymore to say or not. The presence left momentarily.

The next day, their realtor called and said that the sellers were getting quite nervous about selling the home to them because the road was closed right outside of their cul-de-sac, and construction on the lot next door was at a halt. They were going to pull the contract because it was too much of a risk for them. Penelope and Richard were bummed out big time, but still held onto their faith that God would pull them through this somehow. Richard started growing really impatient and frustrated. Penelope told him to calm down and remember God doesn't just make lemonade out of lemons; he gives you the lemonade stand too.

That weekend the wife that owned the house that they'd placed on contract came by and introduced herself. Richard wasn't home, so Penelope was able to talk to her. The woman said it was a shame that the deal couldn't go through and that they seemed like really nice people. However, in view of the road closure and problems with the land next door, she bemoaned the fact that no one knew when it would re-open again. It made sense for them not to sell right then. Penelope assured her that they totally understood and thanked her for coming by to explain in person.

Richard came home shortly after the visit. Penelope explained to him what happened and he was pleasantly surprised that they would come by like that. The kids ran outside to play in the backyard and run around. They'd been having a lot of fun on the big dirt pile in the lot next to them. They'd slide down the huge dirt hill with their winter gliders. Boy, was it a mess to clean up! Penelope couldn't tell which were dirtier, their clothes or shoes, but it seemed worth it for their enjoyment. Penelope was inside cleaning and preparing dinner when she glanced out the back window. On the far right side of the yard, it looked like a dead rabbit was lying on the ground. Shocked, she ran outside to see what it was. She gasped as she approached, "Oh, my gosh! Why is this rabbit dead?"

She looked around to make sure the kids didn't see it but they were running around on the opposite side of the yard, thank goodness. Penelope ran in to tell Richard about the rabbit and he went out and shoveled it into a garbage bag and put it in their trashcan.

Penelope said, "Don't you think that's weird to find a rabbit dead in our yard? We've had several birds die. I know they can hit the windows and stuff like that, but there have been about six birds dead around the outside of the house, one out front, one out back, on the front porch and so on. And now this rabbit."

Richard said, "Yeah, it is kind of strange and creepy. But I'm telling you, we both know it's this house." Penelope then called everyone in to wash up for dinner.

It was evening and time for bed. All the kids were tucked in and as Richard and Penelope were saying their prayers, Penelope received another vision. In the vision she saw a Windermere "For Sale" sign up right in front of Richard's ex-wife's house. It was a sunny day and Penelope could see in her vision the front of the home with the sign hanging in their front yard. The feeling about the vision was that they are definitely going to move, but she just didn't know why. The vision was brief and to the point. She told Richard and of course he grew very curious as to what, where and why would they move.

Richard asked, "Did God tell you why or where they are moving?"

"No, I don't know why, just that they are going to move. They obviously aren't going to move out of state since Michael shares his time with both of you."

Richard said, "I can't stand this, I want to know."

Penelope said, "God doesn't always show everything, but we will see soon enough, I'm sure."

It had been awhile, but they finally had a very restful and peaceful night.

Fourth Year

Four months later.

Fall was transitioning into winter now, so the potential to sell was very slim indeed. Most people were focused on Thanksgiving and Christmas. The project next door finally started and they were erecting a wall around the development as well as the trail system that would run along the south side of their home. The road that was closed had finally opened up after almost a year. The city had to hire a government contractor to come in and re-grade the troubled hillside that collapsed. Alongside the road, they'd added tons of gravel from the top of the hillside down to the bottom to prevent future landslides.

The McAllister's home backed up to a main road and with the construction going on and all of the rain they were getting, water was seeping into their yard. Penelope went down into their crawlspace to make sure they didn't have any kind of flooding issues going on. Upon reaching the crawl space she heard what sounded like a running creek. As she shone the flashlight over to where she heard the sound, sure enough, there was a miniature creek flowing right under their home!

"Oh no!" she gasped. "What the heck! I cannot believe this. This house is a pain in the butt, Richard. You need to come down here and look at this!"

Richard came running into the pantry and leaned down inside as Penelope shone the light for him to see.

"You have got to be kidding me! We can't sell the house with all that water down there, it won't pass inspection. I'll get a hold of someone to fix it and you need to call the city and tell them to come out and fix the back side of our house!"

After several phone calls, it became obvious that the city was going to be political about the run-off. The city informed the McAllister's that several tests had to be performed in dry conditions to determine whether it was their responsibility or the McAllister's to fix it. In the Pacific Northwest there are typically not too many dry days in November, so it would be awhile. A couple of weeks passed, and finally there actually was a dry day, and the city did come by and perform their tests. They established that the run off was, in fact, running into their yard from the city street. While the city workers were investigating their property out back, Penelope asked one of the workers if they knew what was on their property before they built the neighborhood. Apparently, she asked the right worker because he knew all about the Plum Hill area. He leaned on the top of the fence with his forearms and took a deep breath. Then he explained to her that, long before this development and all the others on Plum Hill, it was just a bunch of cow farms.

"Yeah," he said, "I remember those days. All the cows atop this hill and just a few farmers."

Penelope said, "Wow, you must miss those days, huh?"

"Yep, but then I wouldn't have all this work to do, now would I?" He chuckled a little and started to turn around, and Penelope stopped him with one more question. "What was here before the cows and farms?"

The man turned to her again, placed his hand on his chin in thought and said, "This whole area down to the river I believe was Indian territory. I know this particular area on Plum Hill was probably some kind of ritual site."

"Really!" Penelope said.

"Yeah, but that was a very long time ago," he said.

That's all she needed to hear. She thanked God in her mind and turned to the man and thanked him. He then asked her if she'd seen the plans from the city yet. Richard came outside, and the three of them took a look. The plans included a builder for the city installing a proper drain so the runoff would go into a city drain and not their yard. The city would plant trees along the outside of their yard and along the new sidewalk soon to be laid. The sidewalk was a great idea because there wasn't anything in place at all, just a ditch alongside the road. However, the issue regarding the south side of their home, facing the new development, would have to be taken up with the builder if they wanted any kind of privacy on that side.

After reviewing the plans, Richard said to Penelope, "I got a hold of a contractor to fix the crawl space. They said all they need to do is install a sump pump."

"Good! It definitely would pass inspection with all that taken care of. I'll try to reach the builder to see what his plans are for the south side of our home. Hopefully, he'll be willing to work with us."

The next day Penelope ran errands, went running, and then picked Tyler up from preschool. She played with him while preparing for their busy afternoon when the rest of the kids arrived home from school. She happened to look outside and saw workers spray painting orange lines on their property and taking out some of their landscaping!

She ran outside and asked, "What the heck are you doing?" She looked down at the orange lines and saw they were marked pretty far into their yard---probably about six feet wide by twenty feet long! The workers could barely speak English and one of them just said, "You talk to the boss, the boss tell us what to do."

"You tell your boss he can call me about this! In the meantime, you two can get off of our property until this is resolved." The workers looked surprised and intimidated. They quickly walked back to their truck and left.

The next morning, their doorbell rang. Penelope went briskly to the door. As she peeked out the side window it appeared to be either two construction workers or builders standing on their front porch.

She opened the door and said, "Good morning, how can I help you?"

"Hi, is it Mrs. McCallister?"

"Yes," she said hesitantly. "I understand you had a problem yesterday with two of our workers?"

"Yes we did. They were spray painting orange lines inside of our yard."

"Well, you see, ma'am, we measured your lot and it's off about six feet according to our calculations."

"What! I have a copy of our lot on hand and you can take a look if you like."

One of the builders replied, "We don't need to take a look because we have professionals that have already measured. Sometimes the measurements can be off and that's why we had to check with the city first. We will be cutting into your yard according to where the orange marks are located. However, I would be willing to have our workers move your shrubs around for you if you like?"

Penelope responded, "I don't want you moving anything around. That's a lot of shrubs. I want proof that you've got the right measurements."

"Well, you can call the city if you like, ma'am. That's where we received our copy."

"I guess you guys leave us no choice. Thanks for coming by today to explain."

They responded, "No problem, and you have a good day." Penelope closed the door and got on the phone right away to call the city. She was livid and frustrated but was still able to keep her cool. She explained to one of the city planners that not one person informed them of a trail that would be three feet away from their house or that their yard would be invaded forcing them to move their landscaping shrubs. The city planner proceeded to inform her that their records indicate that the builder's property lines are accurate. So the builder has every right to come in and build as he sees fit. Penelope informed the city planner in a facetious tone that she could tell they really care about the people of Peachville, especially with the nice buffer to alleviate encroachment upon private property. There is no way you could tell by looking at the property that the lines were off that much. At least someone could have had the decency to inform them to prepare for the upheaval of their lot.

Richard and Penelope prayed hard that evening. Their patience was growing extremely thin. Even with all of the turmoil going on, their family was sticking together and all the kids still got along great. Once again that night at 2:20 a.m. they were awakened by the bed shaking and this time, as they woke up, the pull strings on their ceiling fan were swinging back and forth directly above their bed. Richard said, ""Do you see that!? Penelope looked up to where Richard was looking and she gasped.

"Richard, we are protected by God," she said, "and I command anything that is not of God to leave in the name of Jesus."

They both lay back down in bed and held hands while trying to go back to sleep. Later in the night, the spirits came back and woke them up by running their 'fingers' up and down their backs from underneath the mattress! They both had chills all over. Richard popped up in bed and said, "Okay, now it's really freaking me out." Just as he said that, their grandmother clock located downstairs in the living room started bonging like crazy. Normally every hour it would ring with a pretty melody, but right now it sounded bizarre, out of control. BING, BONG, POINNNNNG, PING PING BONG BONG BONG!! With each ring it grew louder and louder.

Penelope quickly checked on Tyler and he was fine. They both then rolled toward each other and embraced each other tightly.

"Richard, we have to get out of here."

"I know, baby; don't worry, we'll figure it out."

After a long while, Richard fell asleep, but Penelope was still awake. As she lay in bed thinking and praying, all of a sudden she could see a dark spirit swarming around from the bottom of their bed. It was going for Tyler! She immediately rolled out of bed into Tyler's bed and wrapped her arms over him. As she did this, she swung one arm toward the spirit and commanded it to leave in the name of Jesus. It was a black, short, and squatty circulating spirit. It seemed to be literally turning like a tornado. At the top was a hideous face, slobbering and making a gurgling noise. It had arms that stuck out from the sides of its body as it raced around. It left after she commanded it to leave again, which surprised her. She then slept next to Tyler on his mattress for the rest of the night.

Penelope and Richard woke up really tired the next morning, thinking to themselves that there must be something good that could come out of today. As their morning went on, the builder called and said he changed his mind about how far he would come into their yard. Even though it was his property, he would be willing to only come in halfway so the trail wouldn't be so close to their home, and he would also plant three-foot arborvitae along the south edge of their property for the sake of their privacy. Penelope thanked the builder and hung up the phone. She then jumped for joy. Richard was happy to hear some good news and they both hugged each other, praising God. Richard looked at Penelope and said, "Since it's going to take some time to get out of here, we should invite the church over and have them pray for us."

"You're right," Penelope said. "I'll call and try to explain what we need. I hope they don't think we're crazy."

"Not if you explain right. They've probably had some experience with this kind of stuff, right?"

"Well, I guess we'll find out," she said.

Penelope called their church to see if there was a prayer group experienced enough to come out and anoint their home. After explaining all the details of what was going on, their church was able to gather a group of seven people who were willing to come over and pray. They needed a couple of days to prepare. In the meantime, Penelope made plans for their children to be out of the house during the time the prayer team would come over. Finally after three days of waiting, the prayer group arrived at their home around 7:00 p.m. Penelope and Richard were excited because they truly believed that this prayer team would be able to come in and drive these spirits away.

Everyone came in and sat down in the living room to discuss all issues at hand with Penelope and Richard. One of the men in the group mentioned that you usually encounter these kinds of problems in older homes and was a little surprised that they were having trouble in a newer house. Nonetheless, the team was ready to pray together as a group with Penelope and Richard, and then the plan was for them to go throughout the entire home and anoint it with oil. Penelope kept getting the feeling that some of them in the group either didn't want to be there or didn't take them seriously at all. In some ways she could understand if that was the case.

After their prayer was finished, the team got up from the couch and began walking around their home to pray over it. Each member had a small vial of anointing oil. They would place their finger over the top of the vial and dab a little bit of oil onto their finger and then mark the windows and doorways with the oil in the shape of a cross. As they walked around they asked God to reveal anything to them that was not of him. Two of the women in the prayer group asked if they had any movies or toys that may have opened up a doorway for these spirits to come into their home. There are certain card games or game boards that are meant for evil, and may allow demonic powers to filter into someone's life or home if used in a negative way.

Penelope and Richard both looked at each other and said, "No we don't, but if you are suspicious of anything let us know."

The group then continued to the upstairs of the house and spread out into different rooms, anointing the doorways and windows and praying. Sometimes they would ask each other, if anyone sensed anything? The answer was always no. One of the women from the prayer group did discover some action figure cards that were in the boy's room. She had asked how the boys played with the cards.

Penelope told her, "Michael and Casey never play with those cards the way that game is intended. I didn't know they were considered a "bad" game to play." The woman responded by saying, "Sometimes these types of card games have certain powers behind them if you're not careful, but I don't think these cards are the problem here."

Once the team felt they were done, they told Penelope and Richard that they didn't really find any materialistic things that would "open the doors" for these spirits to come into their home. After being in the home for two hours, the group decided it was time to pray together as a group before they left. As they held hands together in a circle at the top of the stairs, one of the men in the group asked Richard if he had accepted the Holy Spirit.

Richard said, "No, I haven't."

The prayer member suggested that since he is the "head of the household" he should receive the Holy Spirit. Both Richard and Penelope thought that it was kind of odd that they would ask that question right in the middle of trying to battle these evil spirits out of their home. The prayer group concluded their prayers with them and, at that point, Penelope couldn't help but start to cry because she knew the church members weren't able to combat this. The group allowed themselves to become distracted by asking about the Holy Spirit. It was out of line for them to ask Richard something that should be personal between him and God. One of the group members asked if Penelope was okay and she said, yes.

The prayer leader then started to pray that Richard would receive the Holy Spirit right then and there. Penelope could read Richard's body language and could tell that he felt very awkward. Penelope finally said, "This is not working and it's not the right time or place. We appreciate your willingness to come to our home and help."

Richard stepped in and said, "Uh, yeah, thanks for coming by."

The group dispersed and went home.

About two weeks passed following the visit from the prayer team. Penelope received a phone call from one of the women who was part of the prayer group. She had stated to Penelope that a couple of the people from the group said they did see several things in the house during their visit. Penelope was very surprised and relieved because they felt helpless since their church didn't seem to pick up on anything.

Penelope then asked, "Well, what did they see?" The woman stated that they saw two black evil-looking figures in Michael and Casey's room lying on their beds, and then they saw another black tall figure behind the door of Cassandra's bedroom.

"Why didn't you guys tell us at the time?"

The woman simply stated, "We were not prepared for what we saw in your home that night. We were definitely caught off guard and we are not experienced in this area at all. In fact, we have been doing research about incidents like yours that have occurred in England."

"Really? Well, that's too bad you guys didn't know what to do for us then."

The woman responded, "All I can say is we are truly sorry, Penelope, and it wouldn't surprise me at all if you guys wanted to leave the church."

Penelope took a deep breath and said, "Wow, I don't know what to say. We're disappointed and it would have been nice to know that something was discovered when you were here. We have been fighting this for a couple of years now. Did you guys not believe us?"

The woman responded, "Penelope, just know we plan on doing more research on this subject in the hope of helping others who may be experiencing what you guys are. Again, we are really sorry."

Penelope finished their conversation by saying, "I'm not sure what we're going to do but thanks for calling."

Later that evening as Penelope and Richard were talking about the church phone call, Penelope said, "Oh! I forgot to tell you that the realtor called today and said that maybe we should drop the price again, showing the house as a "new listing."

Richard said, "First we had it listed at $585,000! What does she recommend now?"

"She said to drop it by $50,000, so that would $535,000. Considering how much we paid for this house, that's still not a bad investment, other than the guests that came along with the package."

Richard said, "Well, at this point it really doesn't matter; what's important is that we get rid of it."

The next morning everyone was running around getting ready for school. Richard was working in his office. Every day since the house had been listed for sale, Penelope was trying to have the kids pick up after themselves. It was so challenging to keep things perfectly neat with kids, but they were trying their best.

The phone rang and Penelope picked it up. It was her sister's husband on the other line.

"Hey, I hate to be the one to tell you the bad news…" he paused….. "but Amber was unable to tell you herself because she is so upset."

"What happened?"

"Your dad passed away this morning. After your dad got back home from dropping off their grandson, Ritchie, he had another heart attack. I'm really, really sorry."

In shock, Penelope simply stated, "I gotta go Robert, thanks for calling me."

She hung up the phone and ran to the top of the stairs calling down to Richard. "Riiiichharrrd, Riiiichharrrd! Richard!" Richard came to the bottom of the stairs and said, "I was on the phone, what's the matter?"

Penelope could barely say the words, "Mmy, mmyyy, mmyyy dad died this morning. He had a heart attack."

Richard ran up the stairs, wrapped his arms around her, and slowly tightened his hug as they both started to cry.

"Mommy, mommy, what's wrong?" the kids were asking. "What happened? Don't we have to go to school?"

Penelope gained her composure and explained to them what happened. "You guys should still go to school," she said, "because there's not much we can do right now. We will talk about what the plans are when you get home, ok?"

The kids were disappointed because they really thought they'd be staying home and missing school. Penelope was thinking that she needed them to go to school so she could sort out her thoughts. Her dad's doctor was right; dad only had four months left to live. She was at peace knowing she'd spent a lot of quality time on the phone with her dad and she believed he went to heaven.

Richard and Penelope were trying to decide if everyone should go to the funeral or just her. It was a very tough decision to make, but they finally decided the best thing to do was let Penelope go and be with her family. She didn't want the kids to have a stressful visit by traveling all the way to the East Coast for only three days. They'd be faced with family members they hadn't seen in awhile, upset and crying. Richard really wanted to go and support Penelope, but he had to hold down the fort. They really didn't want anyone else to watch the kids with everything going on within their home.

The funeral was planned to take place within four days. Penelope wanted to contribute to the funeral by putting together a picture video, because she knew she wouldn't be able to stand in front of everyone at the ceremony and speak. She would be too upset. Penelope, her brother, Kevin, and his wife, Marsha, would be leaving the next day, so she had to hurry and get this CD together. She made sure there would be a laptop and movie projector for both the "viewing" and the funeral. She thought it would be really nice to have everyone watch the video while talking to people at the viewing. Richard helped her to compile pictures needed for the CD and incorporate the right music. Later that evening as Penelope was working; she sensed that her dad was leaning over her shoulder watching what she was doing. Just as she sensed this, she heard her dad say, "Wow, Pen, that's nice, thank you."

Now, she couldn't see her dad physically, but in her mind she could, and she knew where he was in the room. As she glanced over her shoulder again, her dad said, "Penelope, can you see me!?"

She said, "Yes, but I can't see you with my eyes, only in my mind. I can sense where you are. I can see what your wearing, your face, everything."

Her dad said, "Wow, you have a really neat gift. God has really blessed you." Her dad started to rise and leave through the window. As he did so, he waved to her and said, "I have to go. Love you, daughter," which is what he always said to her. She started to cry but was happy that her dad was at peace. Finishing the CD became even harder after that.

The next morning, Penelope flew back East with her brother and his wife. The CD was completed and ready for the funeral. The kids wanted to go but neither family decided to take their kids for the same reason. The children understood, but would miss their parents more than anything. They arrived safely in Baltimore, Maryland, and drove themselves to their sister, Leslie's, house to stay for the next four nights.

It was wonderful to reunite with the family and help their sister, Leslie, prepare her home for the gathering after the funeral. Everyone helped construct poster boards together by placing pictures of their dad's lifelong snapshots along with written captions. They created three different large poster boards that portrayed their dad's life very nicely. There was an easel that stood holding a framed casing displaying all of the military medals their dad earned while he served in the Army during the Korean War. One of the honors displayed was a purple heart. Their dads' brother, Jan, and his wife, Mary, arranged the ceremony through their church. Volunteers from their church helped serve the gathering at their sister's home, upon their return from the funeral. Their whole family of sisters, brother, nieces, nephews, and Uncle Jan and their mom sat and watched the video in Leslie's basement that Penelope and Richard had created. With the music playing and everyone enthralled with the synchronization of photos, you could hear a pin drop. It was obvious that the group was daydreaming their own memories about him as they watched the collage on screen. When the video was over, Penelope's sister, Sherie, asked, "Where did you find all of the pictures to incorporate into your video?"

Penelope said, "Mom mailed them out to me when Richard and I were planning our wedding because we wanted to create a video for our ceremony, remember?"

"Oh yeeahh. You did a great job; it's going to make everyone cry." Tears appeared in her eyes.

Uncle Jan said, "Wow, I'm impressed. Is this something that will be playing during both the viewing and the funeral?"

Penelope said, "What do you guys think?" Everyone agreed to run it for both events.

Later that evening, while everyone had finished gathering the items needed for the viewing the next day, they were just kind of talking and relaxing. Penelope's brother, Kevin, was walking around in Leslie's basement, perusing her husband's many albums and his stereo system. While Kevin was doing that, Penelope suddenly heard and saw her dad again. She was excited to see him, but also a little leery to show it. She didn't want her family to think she was crazy talking out loud to her dad when she knew they couldn't see him.

As she tried to focus, her dad said, "Can you tell Kevin something for me? I've been trying to talk to him and he can't hear me."

Trying not to look conspicuous, Penelope whispered, "Yes, dad, what is it that you want to tell him?"

"Will you tell Kevin that I love him and I'm very proud of him?"

"Yes, dad, I will" she whispered. Penelope sidled around a bit. As she stared over at her brother, she thought, He's not going to believe this. I mean I think he will, but I don't know if I should tell him now.

Penelope walked around looking at the neat poster boards everyone had worked on, and again, her dad said to her, "Are you going to tell your brother what I said?"

Penelope whispered again with her hand slightly covering her mouth, "Yes, dad, I will, but I don't think right now is the time."

She then pulled her mom to the back of the basement away from everyone else and informed her of what was happening.

Her mom responded, "Penelope, I'm sorry but this is not biblical."

Penelope just looked into her mother's eyes sadly, since she didn't believe her. In Penelope's heart she knew it was from God. She had enough experience throughout her life with these kinds of things to know it wasn't from the "dark side."

Penelope said, "Well, I don't know what to tell you except that dad is here; he is here right now with us and he wants to give each person a message. I figure God is allowing him to do this because he wasn't able to do so prior to his leaving this earth. God can do anything he wants, mom, whether it's biblical or not."

Her mom responded, "Well, I guess you're right about that. You need to be careful, Penelope, and make sure that's what it is."

"Mom, I know what it is. In fact he told me to tell you not to worry and that he loves you very much. With a message like that, how bad could it be?"

Her mom responded in a tired voice, "You could be right about that one too. Come here honey, you need a hug."

The next morning arrived, and there were two viewings scheduled, one in the early afternoon and one later in the evening. Penelope was so not looking forward to this. It was going to be hard to talk to all of those people, and each viewing was about two hours long. She mostly felt bad for her mother, who was exhausted and not feeling well from a bad cold. After a long day, everyone survived the viewings and went back to Leslie's house. Leslie's husband, Dan, owned a successful seafood restaurant. He gave everyone the nicest surprise by having dinner provided for them when they returned. The meal included steamed shrimp, crab cakes etc.… This was a real treat for the families from the Pacific Northwest because seafood out West is… let's just say it lacks the East Coast flair.

The next day came and it was time to go to the funeral. The funeral was at 10:00 a.m. Mom had the very nice idea of having herself and all of the immediate siblings transported in a limousine to and from the funeral. She wanted to splurge. With several of us living far away, who knows when we would all be together again in one place. It was a quiet ride to the ceremony, which was being held at the funeral home. The local paper wrote a very nice article about dad and his family. His father was the mayor of Sykesville for two terms and had accomplished a lot of good things for that small town of Sykesville. They arrived and everyone made sure the poster boards were in place. Uncle Jan did a great job of placing dad's framed medals by his casket. Penelope and Kevin got the computer set up along with the projector and had the CD ready to roll. It was a ceremony filled with lots of love and good messages read out loud from grandchildren and family members. After the second reading, the song, "In the Garden," one of dad's favorites, began playing and Penelope suddenly had the sense that her dad was standing right there in the middle of the sanctuary. She turned around and sure enough he was standing there singing right along, with his chest puffed out with pride like he usually did while he sang. He had on one of his favorite outfits, which was tan kakis and a tan plaid shirt. After the song, it was time for the CD photo show and he stayed to watch it. He looked around the room and said, "This is a really nice ceremony." He then walked through the side window of the sanctuary on a path that was invisible and he slowly faded away.

    Following the ceremony, they all drove to the burial site along with forty other people, including the family members with whom they'd all grown up. It was comforting to have them present. Since dad was in the military, he could have had his burial at the Veteran's Cemetery, but mom and his family already made prearrangements for burial at a family site that was purchased years before. His site would be near his parents, alongside a plot for mom when she passes. Dad's two brothers also had a spot for themselves and their wives. Everyone gathered around under a canopy while mom and the other older family members sat in chairs around one side of the casket. Everyone else stood behind them. There was a bitter cold wind that whipped across the cemetery grounds. It was so cold everyone was shaking and shivering. Army officers performed the folding of the flag ceremony along with the 21-gun salute. The folded flag was then placed into Mom's hands. The officer who placed the flag into her hands told her that not only did dad have one Purple Heart; he was awarded a total of three! Mom started to cry and Penelope placed her hands on her mom's shoulder to comfort her. At that point, Penelope couldn't hold back her tears any longer. The tears streaming down her face felt like they froze on her cheeks it was so bitter cold. Aunt Mary said a prayer aloud and then they all sang, "Jesus Loves Me."

It was time to go back to Leslie and Dan's house to visit and eat with family and friends. There was laughter and tears among the family and friends as they shared their memories. Later that evening, Penelope and her mom were talking in their bedrooms and Penelope could sense her dad's presence again! He didn't really have a message for her, he was just listening. Finally he said, "That's it Pen, let your mom talk and get things out in the open."

Mom was feeling guilty about some things and her dad didn't want her to.

He said something funny: "Now I understand what 'girl talk' is about." Penelope sensed that he stayed with her mom for a while that night.

The next day arrived and before Penelope headed home, she wanted to relay a few more messages. This time it was for her two younger sisters.

She pulled them off to the side and said, "I'm about to tell you something and you may not believe me, but I have to tell you before I leave."

She took a deep breath and said, "Dad has been here during all of the funeral activities, and he would like me to share with you a message."

They looked at her and listened. "Dad loves you both and he wants the best for you. He apologizes for not always being there. He wants you to know he tried to show how much he loves you by supporting you during the times in your life when you faced some difficult situations."

They both understood and tried not to cry. Penelope wished so much that she could stay longer; but, unfortunately, it was time to head back West with Kevin and Marsha. She knew she had to tell her brother his message from dad. Perhaps on the plane would be a good place to discuss it. As they sat on the plane, she finally brought up the subject. She looked over at Kevin and said, "Do you remember when everyone was helping with the pictures?"

Kevin was sitting in his seat easing the weariness with his eyes closed. He said, "Mmmm-hmmmm."

"Well, you may not believe me, but dad was in the room with us."

Kevin opened his eyes, looked over at Penelope, leaned forward and said, "He what?"

With her eyes wide open she nodded her head, "He was with us in Leslie and Dan's basement. He was trying to talk to you but you couldn't hear him so he asked me to tell you something."

Kevin was really interested now, sitting up straight. He said, "I believe you, what did he have to say? I feel bad I didn't know he was there."

"It's okay, Kevin. He said for me to tell you that he loves you and he's very proud of you."

Kevin sat back and soaked in what his sister just told him and then said, "That's really cool you can see those things and receive messages. I wish I could talk to him. I would have talked…."

"I know, Kevin."

Kevin said, "What's my gift?"

She answered, "Are you kidding me?! You have the ability to meet someone for the very first time and know if they are being honest---if they're good people. It takes me a few times being around them before I would pick up on that."

Kevin said, "Yes, I can do that, but it would be really cool if I could do what you do."

In a comforting tone, Penelope said, "Well, God is the one who picks each of the gifts that he feels fits us best. Trust me; sometimes I don't see good things. Your gift serves you well being a police officer."

Kevin said, "Yea, I guess you're right, Pen."

They made it home safely and everyone got dropped off at home. Penelope was greeted by the kids and Richard at the door with lots of hugs and kisses! Tyler was in the kitchen and he pointed toward the front door and said, "Look, Pom Pom!" There was no one standing by the front door and Pom Pom is Richard's dad.

Penelope and Richard looked at each other confused, and Richard said, "You know I was going to say that it feels like your dad is with us. It feels like he walked in with you tonight."

"Really?" Penelope said.

Again, Tyler said, "Mommy, there's Pom Pom, look!"

Penelope picked Tyler up and said, "You see Pom Pom?"

Again Tyler pointed toward the front door smiling. She gave Tyler a kiss on his cheek and put him back down.

Richard said, "Why does he keep saying its Pom Pom?"

Penelope said, "He must think my dad looks a little like your dad. If you think about it, they are similar in their looks."

Richard said, "Yeah, I guess you're right."

Penelope then proceeded to tell Richard all about the trip and how she saw her dad and the messages.

Richard said, "Wow, that is cool! God must be allowing him to come here and talk with you. I'm glad he's here."

Everyone went to bed… And all too soon Penelope was reminded of the unwanted guests in their home. It was another night of shenanigans. The bed shook, waking them up again. Penelope saw her dad by their bedroom door. He said, "I can't come in because there is something dark and evil here. I'll come back another time."

Penelope was sad, but too tired to not go back to sleep. Richard went downstairs to sleep again.

The next day, Richard and Penelope were discussing their house situation and decided to go through a different realtor. They had the "For Sale" sign taken down and another analysis done. This time the realtor suggested some changes in furniture placement and brought the price down in hopes of selling faster. He was pretty optimistic about selling it, which made Richard and Penelope feel better. They never heard anything from their previous realtor. At least with new pictures and a fresh look, their "New Listing" would have some hope.

Penelope was looking over some of the house paperwork in her office and all of a sudden, out of the corner of her eye, she saw her dad standing there. "Dad!"

"Hey Pen, can you call your mother today and tell her that I love her and that everything will be okay?"

"Sure, dad, I will do that. I love you, dad, and I miss you already."

He said, "I love you too," and he slowly walked away. Somehow Penelope knew she would see him again. Of course she did not hesitate. She called her mom and told her the message. This time her Mom was a lot more open-minded to what she was saying. After she got off the phone with her mom, the phone rang.

"Hello?"

"Hi Penelope, this is Pat from the prayer group."

Hearing from Pat really threw Penelope for a loop. They'd left their church after the praying incident because they felt abandoned. It had probably been about six months now. Even though they were attending a different church, they didn't have the same warm feeling they had enjoyed at their home church.

"Hi Pat, how are you?"

"Good, hey listen, I just wanted to tell you that I've been praying for you and your family. I'm really hoping that God would just burn down your house altogether because I really feel that is the only way to get rid of those spirits."

Penelope said, "Well, I never thought of it that way, but that would be nice because I really don't know when we are going to sell and we can't just leave right now. We're kind of forced to fight this out until we can move."

Pat said, "Penelope, you know you're not going to win, right?"

She answered, "I guess it just makes me feel better to fight. This is our home and I really don't want to move. This is our first home together."

"I can totally understand all of that," said Pat, "but you must leave and soon."

"I know, Pat."

"You and your family are protected, Penelope. You know that, right?"

"Yes, I have faith that God won't let anything happen, but I also feel the urgency to get things moving."

"Good. You need to do that. I just wanted to call and make sure everything is okay and to let you know you can rely on the prayer group to support and pray for your family."

"Awww, thanks so much, Pat. We really appreciate that; you have no idea."

"Cheerfully, Pat said, "Hopefully we'll see you and your family come back to our church soon."

"Okay Pat, thanks again."

It was hard to believe Christmas time had arrived already. This year it was hard because it made Penelope think of her mom having her first Christmas without dad. It sure made her miss her family back East so much. Richard and Penelope figured they probably wouldn't sell their home until spring now. The house was fully decorated and, as the kids and Penelope decorated the tree, they listened to Christmas music and ate their infamous Italian cookies. The Italian cookie recipe went way back to when Penelope was a little girl. Her best friend's grandmother was from Italy and used to make these cookies every year for her family. She was nice enough to hand down the recipe to Penelope's mom. These cookies were the best, all different Christmas cutouts with white frosting and different sprinkles atop. Richard and Penelope started a tradition that every Christmas, each child got to buy a new ornament from the store with which they would decorate the tree. When they grew up and had their own place they would have some nice tree ornaments. While everyone was humming Christmas songs and decorating and eating, Penelope happened to glance out the front window and she saw the tip of their fir tree being pulled all the way down to the ground!

"What the heck?" she said. Then she saw Richard pulling on a string of lights that apparently didn't work. He was trying to pull the string of lights off the tree and the tree was winning. Richard grabbed the lights by the end and yanked on that tree in a tizzy fit, pulling it back and forth. The tree was literally bent all the way down to the ground. She could only imagine what words were coming out of that man's mouth, probably something very similar from the dad in the movie, "The Christmas Story." Penelope opened up the front door and started laughing at Richard. "Wow, how old *are* you?"

Richard's face slowly went from frustration to a big smile. Penelope and the kids finished trimming the tree. It was beautiful with all the kids' decorations, red lights and a lit-up angel as the topper. The tree stood by the window so you could see the lights from the street. Even with all of these weird happenings, their home felt cozy and warm.

Spring arrived…

Penelope and Richard were becoming a bit desperate to leave their home. They started looking at homes for sale all through their small town. They had decided to move out when they found something and then try to sell their home later. There were quite a few homes for sale. At this point, they almost didn't care what part of town it was in, just as long as it would fit. Richard and Penelope did a lot of praying together. Each time they saw a home they would pray, "Is this the home for our family, Lord?"

So far, they hadn't received a "yes." All the kids enjoyed going house shopping together. Surprisingly, a lot of the homes had cookies or some treats out that the kids could enjoy while mom and dad looked around the house. In each house that they looked at, the kids would run to each of the bedrooms and pick out which one they would claim as their own. Cassandra needed a room to herself since she was the only girl. Then Casey would run to the biggest room and Michael would follow him. Tyler would run in with the boys and they would tell him that his room was next to theirs. Tyler would say, "No, I'm with you guys, right?"

Casey would hold onto Tyler and say, "You go to bed before we do, so you go in there, but you can come in our room anytime you want, ok?" Tyler would get a big smile on his face and dance around.

Even though they hadn't found a home yet, Penelope started to pack their things in boxes and prepare so they could move out quickly. They definitely would have enough items for an estate sale. Penelope started listing items she knew they wouldn't keep and placed them online to sell.

As she prepared their things, she prayed to God, "Which things should we keep and which ones should we not keep?" God guided her through the entire process.

She wanted to keep some of the furniture for her decorating business, but with everything going on she didn't know if there would be enough space to store everything. Her business was starting to take off a bit. After each project she finished, God always brought another customer her way. She was glad it wasn't full-time yet because she loved being home for the kids and Tyler was still in preschool.

Richard received an unexpected call from Pastor Frank. "Hi, Richard, how are you guys?" Richard explained to Pastor Frank what was going on.

Pastor Frank said, "I heard about the prayer group coming out to your house. How about I come out and pray with you and Penelope?"

Richard thought that would be a great idea so they scheduled a time for him to arrive. After Richard hung up the phone, he couldn't wait to tell Penelope. "You are not going to believe this! Pastor Frank is going to come over and pray for us and take a look around our house."

"Wow, that's great! Penelope cheered. "I hope when he comes over he will be able to pick up on what's here. I don't know about you, Richard, but I'm still moving. I mean, God would really have to use Pastor Frank in a mighty way for me to change my mind."

Richard said, "Oh no, we *are* still moving. We cannot live in here anymore. I just think it would be nice to have Pastor Frank over."

Penelope said, "I totally agree. It's great that he would even want to come over, knowing what we have going on."

Pastor Frank arrived at their home in the middle of the day while the kids were at school. They all three sat in the living room just talking a little bit about everything but their house situation.

Finally Pastor Frank said, "Let's pray." He prayed for God to watch over Richard, Penelope and their family.

When he finished, he paused and then said, "You know God is more powerful than Satan, right?"

Penelope said, "Yes, we do."

He continued, "Well, then whatever is here does not have authority over you or your home, and you should not be afraid. Don't be afraid."

"Pastor Frank, we agree with you on that," said Penelope, "but sometimes I think there might be footholds that allow Satan to keep his power."

"What do you mean by that?" asked Pastor Frank.

"I mean ultimately God does have authority over everything on this earth, but sometimes if there was an event that took place on a property or within a home, depending upon what that may be, it could allow the power of evil to remain there."

Pastor Frank asked, "What kind of event are you talking about, Penelope?"

She cleared her throat. "I'm talking about a ritual of some kind that may have taken place on this property that would allow this to continue."

Pastor Frank interjected, "But again, God has the authority over those powers."

She said, "Then why won't they leave, Pastor Frank? Richard and I have prayed over this home, we have blessed our house numerous times; the prayer group has even come out and anointed our house. We have marched around our home on the outside and asked God to bless our property, and we have searched from the attic down to the crawlspace to see if there were any kinds of satanic or ritual markings that may have been left behind. We have searched for any clues that would cause this and the only thing that we have discovered is that this land was a place for Indian rituals that may have involved sacrifices of some kind. Usually when you suspect that an object has a curse on it or something 'bad' over it, you can burn it and get rid of it that way. But, I'm not sure what you do when it's property."

Pastor Frank was listening intently and said, "Well, my wife and I had issues at our other home we used to live in and it would come and go and we would pray against it. Eventually we moved, but that's *not* the reason why we moved. We knew that God was protecting us and when we told it to leave, it left. I believe if you tell it to leave, it will go."

Penelope said, "I understand what you mean, pastor, but this is a bit different."

Richard then said, "Frank, maybe if you take a walk upstairs and have a look around you'll see what we're talking about."

Pastor Frank stood up, adjusted his shirt around his waistband. He then stood there looking at Richard.

Richard said again, "Go ahead, and feel free to look around. We can come up with you or we'll just stay down here so you can do your thing."

Pastor Frank's face turned red and he looked at Penelope, then at Richard and said, "Which way would you like me to leave?"

Penelope and Richard looked at each other puzzled. Richard said, "What, what do you mean?"

Pastor Frank said, "How do you want me to leave?"

Penelope then said, "I guess the same way you came in."

Richard opened the front door for Pastor Frank and the two of them had a brief conversation that had nothing to do with why he was there and then Pastor Frank left. Richard closed the door slowly and he and Penelope looked at each other in disbelief.

Richard said, "That's so weird that he wouldn't go upstairs. I guess he just wasn't ready for this kind of work."

Penelope said, "He must have sensed it and realized he was in way over his head." Feeling a little abandoned, Penelope and Richard hugged each other. Richard kissed her forehead and said, "Don't worry baby, we will find a house and get the heck out of here."

The holiday weekend arrived and everyone was looking forward to sleeping in and playing around outside. Penelope's brother and his wife, Marsha, stopped by to pick up some things and say hello.

Her brother asked how everything was going.

"Well, pretty good other than trying to sell this house and getting the heck out of here." They both laughed.

She said, "Hey, why don't you guys stay for lunch?"

"Nah," he said, "we've got baseball practice and Jamie has soccer. Sorry, Pen, I feel like we never see each other because we're so busy."

Penelope just smiled and said, "I understand. We should get together more often though."

Kevin was looking upstairs and he glanced over at Penelope. "So you're still having problems with all that stuff?" Penelope nodded and just shrugged her shoulders. "Would you mind if I took a look upstairs?"

"Of course not, by all means, do have a look," Penelope said.

Richard said, "Enter at your own risk." Everyone started laughing.

Marsha said, "I'll go up and take a look around." Kevin stayed downstairs and waited for Marsha. As Marsha came down the stairs her face was flushed and her eyes were wide open.

"Is everything okay, Marsha?" Penelope asked.

Marsha replied, "I'll tell you, it's been a long time since I had the hair on my arm stick straight up like this," and she showed everyone her arm. She continued, "There is definitely something upstairs and it gave me the creeps. It felt like something was watching me. Funny thing is, I did feel something in Tyler's room, but it was really strong in your bedroom."

Penelope said, "Yes, that's mainly where all of the action is now. Tyler is sleeping in our room now, which probably explains that."

Kevin looked over at Penelope and said, "Awww, that's too bad."

Richard looked over at Kevin and said, "Are you going to go up and check it out?" Kevin then walked up to the top of the stairs, paused for a moment and then turned right around and came back down quickly.

Richard asked him, "Are you alright? It's kind of creepy, huh? Are you scared?"

Kevin said, "No I'm not scared", and then his face turned red. Penelope gasped slowly and said, "You are scared. Awwww, it's okay, Kevin. I don't blame you for feeling that way; it's pretty powerful stuff up there."

Kevin was feeling a little awkward. Marsha said, "Well, on that note we'd better get going so Zach's not late for practice."

Penelope said, "Okay, guys, great to see you, as always."

Kevin and Marsha gave everyone a warm and comforting hug. They wished they could do more.

Summer time arrived…

Summer came with its awesome display of beautiful flowers and aromas, frogs croaking, crickets and warm sun, which was much missed during the winter months in the Northwest. The garden was doing so well this year and so were the hanging baskets along the front porch. The flowers on their front porch had been attracting a lot of hummingbirds. It was nice to watch them flutter around the blossoms.

The kids were playing outside while mom was getting some odds and ends done around the house. She walked down the hallway by the laundry room, and out of the corner of her eye, she saw Cassandra with her long dark brown curly hair. She was wearing a white dress and staring out the window. As she continued past the laundry room, she said, "Hi Cassandra," and then walked downstairs, thinking that she must have gotten that white dress from the dress-up box. She thought to herself, ...*a little weird how she was staring out the window.* She reached the kitchen and Cassandra was standing there drinking a glass of water. And she did not have a white dress on!

Surprised, Penelope said, "Oh! You're in the kitchen? I thought I just saw you upstairs."

Cassandra chuckled and said, "No mommy, I just came in from outside to get a drink, it's getting hot out there."

Cassandra then set her glass on the kitchen counter and said, "I'm going back outside, mom!"

"Okay honey, have fun!" Penelope's stomach did flip flops and that alarming feeling shot through her body. She could not believe that she thought that thing was Cassandra in the laundry room! She took a minute to catch her breath, looked up the stairs and started to pray for protection over their family. It happened every time. Just when she thought she could relax…just when she felt that nothing crazy was happening around the house, she would get caught off guard with another bizarre event. What concerned her most is how events were happening during the day as well as the evening.

Casey came inside from playing and decided to go up into Tyler's room to lie on his box spring and rest a minute. After all, he wasn't sleeping in there anymore and it was a shorter walk to Tyler's room than his. As he was lying on the box spring, he felt like something was watching him. He raised his head up to look around and didn't see anything. He then laid his head back down on the pillow and took a deep breath and released it. Right at that point, a dark figure leaned in over his face and yelled, "Get out! You're interfering!"

Casey immediately jumped off the box spring, stopped by the doorway and took a quick glance back into the room. Once again he heard, "Get Out!" He ran into his own room, then went back outside.

Later that evening, Casey told his mom what happened. She told Casey to tell her right away when things like that happen. She asked him, "Are you okay? Nothing else happened to you did it?"

"No mom, it was just weird. I'm okay."

It had been quite the day and Penelope was definitely ready to open up a bottle of wine with dinner and relax a bit. Richard was busy, as usual, and he sure didn't mind sitting down with Penelope and enjoying a glass himself. After everyone finished their dinner, they took showers, finished watching their movie together and then went to bed.

The next morning Richard came into the kitchen and said, "You know, I have a lot of work to get done for my trip coming up next week. Why don't you take the kids to the beach and spend the night?"

Excited she said, "Really!? That sounds awesome!" Then she stood there for a second and said, "But it doesn't feel right."

He said, "What do you mean? I'm telling you to take the kids to the beach and you, of all people, would be all over that."

She said, "You're right, but for some reason, it just doesn't feel right to me this time."

He said, "Then just go for the day." Penelope stood there and thought how much the kids would really love that, so she gave in and they packed their things and left for the beach. On the way, one of the main highways was closed for a running event.

"Shoot! I don't know my way around this one, guys." She was horrible with directions so they traveled around the city for an hour!

Finally, Penelope called Richard almost in tears, "I cannot believe I can't find my way around this stupid highway!"

Frustrated, Richard said, "Penelope! Are you serious? I don't know what to tell you. Just ask someone and then call me when you guys get there."

After hanging up the phone, she was determined to get everyone to the beach. She looked at her children through the rear view mirror and said, "I guess we'll get there when we get there. We already wasted an hour driving around."

Casey and Cassandra said, "Mom just take us to the zoo! We don't care if we go to the beach or not."

Tyler was just smiling in his car seat. Penelope was thinking how messed up this was. Are you trying to speak to me, God? They finally made their way to the beach. She was thinking that the kids needed a break and it would be so much fun to go run on the beach and play around. They checked into their little hotel and walked down to the beach and played around for two hours. The kids did love it and had fun. After that, it was time to head back to the room and then go have some dinner. They walked into this really quaint Mexican restaurant and ordered dinner to go. As they walked back to their hotel, Penelope could not explain this feeling of uneasiness, almost like they should not be there. She was under stress from the house and could kick herself for not listening to her instincts from the beginning. Even the kids had given her hints of what to do, sheesh! She said a short prayer in her mind as they were walking, *God, please protect us in the name of Jesus.*

They walked through the doorway of the hotel and sat down, turned the TV on, and watched a kid's movie together. As they were watching the show, someone tried to come into their room! The door was chained so the door banged open with only the chain preventing the man from entering. He tried to open it again and Penelope yelled, "You got the wrong room, mister!" He slammed the door shut and then they could hear him say, "Sorry, I guess I had the wrong room." He and another man walked off.

The four of them looked at each other and Penelope tried to keep things calm and said, "Let's finish watching our show. Don't worry; everything is okay, guys." She could tell that the two men weren't trying to harm them, but it did scare her.

As the night went on, that eerie feeling came back again and she wondered if the kids could feel it as well. They were deciding who was going to sleep in what bed and then Casey said, "Mom, we need to leave and we need to leave now."

Penelope took a deep breath and thought, Oh Lord, please help us. I'm sorry I didn't understand you on this one. We are going to go home. Cassandra kind of wanted to stay, but Tyler said, "Let's go home, mommy."

Penelope thought she would never hear them wanting to go back to that house, how ironic! Penelope looked at her watch, sheesh! It was 11:00 p.m.! "Well, let's go for it, get your things together, leave the food here. I'll leave the key at the hotel door."

Casey couldn't move any faster; that boy helped everyone get together and into the van quickly. Of course the plan was to fuel up in the morning. The tank was very low, lower than a quarter! *Okay, God, this is where you kick in. We need to make it to the gas station that's right after the pass, which is about 54 miles out!* There were a couple of places she could check before they totally left all of the beach towns. Everything was closed. She decided not to waste anymore time or gas. Off they headed toward home. On the way home she was gripping the steering wheel, begging God to let them make it to the gas station on the other side of the pass. She was then thinking to herself, what kind of mother am I? I have three beautiful children in the car and we might get stranded in the middle of nowhere! No, that's not what's going to happen! I am going to have faith in you, Lord, and I know you will get us out of here safely. She then looked up to the sky and there was a huge beautiful bright full moon, which lit up the sky and the road. It was almost as if God was holding a flashlight leading the way. It was absolutely gorgeous. She could feel peace settle upon them. Casey and Tyler fell asleep. Cassandra stayed up a bit and kept her mom company. At one point along the highway they saw the biggest elk ever! It was like the mighty keeper of the forest looking out from around all of the huge tall pine trees to see who would dare come through his woods at that hour of night. They finally reached the gas station and the manager was just getting ready to close! Penelope jumped out of the car and told him that she was out of gas and would he please let her fill up. He was a very slim man with a long gray beard, long hair and he appeared very tired. They both locked eyes for a few seconds and he said yes, even though he didn't want to.

Penelope said, "May God bless you today, sir. Thank you so much!!"

He hesitated for a second, and then turned around, shook his head slightly and walked back inside of the mart. She definitely felt better with a full tank of gas and familiar highways ahead of them. Now everyone was asleep. Penelope was having a debate in her mind about whether or not to call Richard. He slept so horrible, she figured if she woke him he wouldn't be able to go back to sleep, but then again, he may wonder who was coming into the garage. Well, duh, if someone was opening up the garage, it obviously would be her. So she decided not to call and went home. Upon arrival it was 1:00 a.m. and Casey and Cassandra woke up. Penelope held Tyler in her arms and the other two walked with her into the garage quietly. As they opened the door inside of the garage, Richard had already awakened up and was standing behind the door prepared to kick their butts with a 3-foot-long massage stick. The stick was cocked above his head ready to wreak wrath upon the intruders. Once he realized it was his family, his aggressive anger disappeared into a sigh of relief and he lowered the stick.

Casey said, "Daddio, it's us!"

Cassandra said, "Sheesh daddio, what did you think we were, robbers?"

Penelope stood there speechless with her mouth hanging open.

Richard started to calm down and said, "What the heck? Why didn't you call?"

Penelope filled him in with the whole story and he hugged everyone. Everyone got settled into their beds. As Richard and Penelope lay in bed, he said, "You know I'm really glad you guys came home because I was being attacked big time. I mean I really felt like I wouldn't have made it through the night. I tried to sleep downstairs and they bothered me down there. I then went upstairs and the bed was shaking and it wouldn't leave. I've been terrified all night. Thank God you're here."

Penelope said, "Awww, now I know why God didn't want us staying at the beach. He was trying to scare us to come back for your sake." She went to sleep and snored all night because she was so tired. Richard didn't care; he just snuggled up to her anyway. Everyone slept very well that night.

The next day everyone just hung around playing in the pool in the backyard and eating popsicles. It was a nice day to hang out on the front porch and read a good book. After dinner, Richard treated everyone to frozen custard. Their family loved the frozen custard place. Summertime was always fun and relaxing. In another week, it would be time for Casey and Cassandra to visit their dad in Michigan for three weeks. Michael would also go to his mom's for three weeks. Penelope was only looking forward to this because of what was going on in the house. She was glad for them to go have some fun while she and Richard tried to figure out what to do. Plus it gave them some one-on-one time with Tyler.

It was evening and time for bed. All the kids were so tired, no one complained once about going to bed. After watching their show together, Penelope and Richard headed upstairs for bed. Penelope was not even all the way asleep when she suddenly felt the bed shaking and then something abruptly bumped into their bed. She tapped Richard to see if he was feeling the same thing. He was asleep. She whispered, "It figures. Get out in the name of Jesus. I command you to leave right now, you are not welcome here!"

The bed stopped shaking and she went back to sleep. Then they both were awakened, this time by Casey moaning. He was having another bad dream.

Richard said, "You better go in there before he gets louder and he wakes everyone up."

Penelope let out a deep breath and walked into Casey's bedroom. When she arrived, she asked, "Did you have that bad dream again?"

He nodded his head and said, "This time it was different but still really weird. Mom, I'm scared, I don't like this house anymore."

"Me either, sweetie. Don't you worry, Daddio and I will find another house that doesn't scare any of us, ok?"

"Okay mom."

"Now try and go back to sleep." She leaned over and kissed his forehead. As she walked back into her bedroom, Richard said,

"Well, that does it for me; downstairs I go. Just try to sleep, honey, I don't want to toss and turn and bother you."

She said, "Don't worry, you're not bothering me. I don't want you downstairs."

"Well, I have to. Sorry." He turned in frustration and headed for the stairs.

Penelope listened to Richard's footsteps go all the way downstairs and she longed for him to stay with her in bed. Slowly she went back to sleep. Casey woke up again, and this time he ran to his mom's bedroom and climbed into bed with her. His mom wrapped her arms around him and let him snuggle with her. In the morning, Richard walked upstairs and glanced in their bed and said, "What's he doing in here?"

Surprised by his comment, Penelope said, "Do you really need that explained to you? He was scared again. It's getting a lot worse in here."

Richard said, "I know, maybe we can look at some more houses when I get back from my trip."

She said, "That would be great! I could also look while you're gone."

"Yeah, then if you find something, we could look at it together when I get back."

"Good idea, babe."

Of course the whole time Richard was gone, Casey wanted to sleep in their room and since he was sleeping in their room, Cassandra and Michael wanted to come in too. So their mom pulled another mattress into their bedroom so they all could sleep together.

The next day, Penelope walked up to the mailbox and their neighbor, Tracy, was getting her mail too.

Tracy said, "Hi Penelope!"

"Hey Tracy, how are you?"

"We're good, busy with work and running the girls around. Hey, we're going to the beach for the Fourth of July. Do you think you could water the flower pots for me again?"

Penelope said, "Oh sure, no problem at all."

Tracy paused for a second and said, "You know, I've been meaning to ask you, How *is* the house doing?"

"What do you mean?" Penelope said.

Hesitantly Tracy answered, "Well, I really didn't want to tell you this and I kind of felt bad not telling you sooner, but the family who lived in the house before you had some issues."

Penelope eyes widened. "What do you mean? What kind of issues."

"Their youngest son used to play outside with our girls. One time while they were all playing he killed a rabbit and thought it was funny. I never let my girls play with him again. That wasn't the only incident either. He killed several rabbits and other animals. I always thought there was something wrong with the house for him to act that way. He just acted really strange."

With some relief, Penelope felt she could talk about this with Tracy. "I have to tell you, Tracy," she said, "the house is not fine. We are having a lot of issues going on and that's why we want to move. All of us are being bothered in the night and I think if we didn't have God protecting us, Tyler would probably have the same issues as that little boy did."

Tracy nodded her head. "Penelope, we have something in our basement as well. It doesn't come around all of the time, just once in awhile and when it does, the girls won't go down there at all to play. We all can feel its presence. We even had a priest and a psychic come in to try and get rid of it for us."

Penelope said, "How did that work out for you?"

"Well, it didn't go away, but like I said, it's only sometimes."

Penelope asked her, "How can you live there with that presence?"

"I guess we have just gotten used to it, but I can understand why you want to move."

Penelope informed Tracy that the spirits' hold may have something to do with the land. She asked, "I wonder if anyone else has issues?"

Tracy said, "I do believe it could be the land because all of this was Indian ground. I don't know if anyone else has issues but maybe."

With relief, Penelope said, "Tracy, thanks for sharing that with me, it all makes sense now, and don't feel bad for not telling us. Not everyone is open to what we're talking about."

"Well, I'm open about it. I totally believe that kind of stuff is real. If you ever need to talk about it, give me a call, okay?"

"I will Tracy, thanks again, and don't worry, I'll take care of your garden while you're gone."

It was time to say goodbye to Casey and Cassandra for a few weeks while they visited their dad in Michigan. They had all kinds of plans to go swimming, boating, fishing and camping. They always had a good time with their dad. Michael was off to his mom's and their plans were to visit Disney World. He was really excited about that because they were staying at a place where the animals were enclosed right in the middle of the property where their hotel was. When the older three left, it was extra quiet and Tyler missed them, but he also liked having all of the attention too.

It was Fourth of July weekend, and time to walk over to Tracy's house and water everything for her. Boy, was it a hot summer. Without proper watering, her plants and flowers would have shriveled up to dust. As Penelope was watering, a storm breeze was brewing, and she had the sense that it was not going to be a quiet evening in more ways than one. She quickly gathered up the hoses and locked things up.

She, Richard and Tyler had a nice dinner together out back while the winds increased but nothing threatening as of yet. After cleaning up the kitchen, the lightning started and it grew black outside. She and Richard made sure everything was tied down outside and closed up all of the windows and the garage. CRAAACK! went the thunder, it felt like it was coming down the street. The power went out, and Penelope and Richard gasped. Strong thunderstorms usually happen on the East Coast, not in the Pacific Northwest. All three of them were kind of scared because they did not want to be in the house without power. There was so much lightning that you really didn't need a flashlight; it lit up everything and came with loud pealing thunder that rumbled through the valley. Penelope ran upstairs to light some candles because it was starting to get really dark outside, while Richard held Tyler in his arms. She lit three large pillar candles that were hanging above their Jacuzzi tub. The master bathroom leads right into their bedroom so they could see when they all came to bed. She then went back downstairs to light a couple of freestanding candles so they could see while they were downstairs. Richard had already grabbed a flashlight and used that to walk around with Tyler so he didn't trip over anything. The crackling and pealing thunder now crashed right over their house; they could feel the house shake! It was so powerful it made all three of them jump. They decided to sit outside on the bench underneath the covered front porch. They could not bear to stay in the house anymore with the storm raging. They were cuddled up tightly on the bench together. Tyler was holding on for dear life in his mom's lap. Penelope suddenly had a sense that something was not right in the house. Both she and Richard felt like the spirits were staring at them through the window of the front door. The feeling was so intense that Penelope said she would go in and make sure everything was okay in the house. She placed Tyler on Richard's lap and reluctantly went inside of the house with a flashlight in hand. Sure enough, spirits were everywhere! She could feel every strand of hair on her body sticking straight up. There was a very strong feeling that she was surrounded. She felt the urgency to go upstairs and check on things. When she reached their master bathroom, one of the three candles had burned all the way down to nothing! The wax from the candle had spilled out of the holder, down the wall, and all over the counter of the tub! She gasped loudly and immediately blew out the other two candles. She ran downstairs and back outside to Richard and Tyler.

Richard said, "Are you alright?"

Penelope quickly said, "No, it's really weird. One of the candles upstairs totally melted all over the place."

He said, "What? What do you mean?"

"When we decide to go back in, you'll have to see for yourself. I have never had a candle do that before."

Finally the storm subsided and they all three went back inside.

Penelope said, "Let's get Tyler tucked in bed and then I can show you the candle." Richard walked into their bathroom while Penelope was tucking Tyler into bed and shone the flashlight on the candles and couldn't believe it either.

"How long were we sitting on the porch?" Richard asked.

She answered with a tired voice, "Maybe a half-hour, forty five minutes at the most." Out of curiosity Richard asked, "How tall was the candle?"

"It's as tall as the other two candles, about twelve inches high and six inches wide." He said, "Well, I think somebody was having fun in here while we were sitting on the porch and I think they were trying to start a fire or something."

Penelope said, "It's so weird."

The power stayed off the whole night. All three slept in the same bed that night.

The next morning Penelope was regretting the fact that Richard had a two-day business trip coming up, which meant it would be just she and Tyler alone in their haunted house. *At least it's only for one night,* she thought.

The evening before Richard's business trip, he thought it would be nice to take the three of them out to dinner to one of their favorite places, Little Italy Tratitoria. They offered the best Italian food and coffee. While sitting in the restaurant, Penelope said, "I really don't want you to leave. Tyler and I will be searching for a house while you're gone."

Richard said, "Oh, you'll be okay. Remember, God is watching over you guys. If you're feeling that uncomfortable, maybe you should call my mom and dad and ask if you could stay over there."

She said, "No, I don't want to go over there. I feel like they don't fully believe us."

Richard said in a calming voice, "I know what you mean, but they wouldn't mind. It's better than staying alone in our house."

In a sad voice she said, "I'm going to miss you, Richard."

Richard left the next morning and Penelope was thinking maybe it wouldn't be too bad because they'd enjoyed a good sleep the past couple of nights. They kissed goodbye and she got Tyler ready to search around town for a home. It was easy to take Tyler because he loved looking at houses and pulling the flyers out of the realtor box for his mom. "Hey Tyler, I will treat you to Burgerville when we're done, okay?"

"Cheeseburber!" He was smiling from ear to ear.

They started from Snowy Mountain where her brother lived and looked all around until they hit town again and headed down toward the river. She made no appointments because she wanted to find the 'right' house first. They were able to look at some "Open Houses" so Tyler could get out and walk around too. Penelope was praying all day long, "God help us find the right home and please protect all of us while we are away from each other in the name of Jesus, Amen!"

Tyler said, "Amen!"

They searched for hours and finally stopped to get lunch. Penelope was disappointed because she really thought they would have found something by now. Nothing felt right and there weren't any real answers from God yet. She looked at Tyler and said, "You know what? Since you have been so good driving around helping mommy find a house, I'm going to take you swimming."

"Yeaaahhhhh! Thank you, mommy!" They went to their community swimming pool and had a good hour and a half of swimming and playing and then went home.

Upon returning home, they fixed dinner and played some games. Penelope then went upstairs to throw their pool wear into the washer. When she came back downstairs, Tyler was walking around. He looked at his mom and said, "Mommy, we need to weave and we need to weave now."

Penelope could feel the strong presence, which again felt like they were being surrounded. It was cold and her hair stood straight up. She knew in her heart if they stayed, it would not be a good outcome for them. It was getting closer to evening, which meant they didn't have much time to diddle-daddle. She called her brother and asked him if they could stay at his house. He and his family were out of town but he said they could if they wanted to.

He asked her, "Are you okay?"

"Yes, it's just Tyler and me home and we're really scared."

"Awww, Pen I wish we were there for you. You know where the key is, just go up and make yourself at home, ok?"

"Okay, thanks so much Kevin!"

Kevin said, "We'll talk to you later."

Penelope and Tyler made their way back up to Snowy Mountain and got settled in. She definitely felt safe there. Her brother's two dogs kept running around on the deck outside that surrounded the house. They were barking up a storm, which freaked Penelope out. Tyler on the other hand, fell asleep and stayed that way all night.

The next morning, they packed up their things, had breakfast and planned on going home when Richard returned, which would be around 4:00 p.m.

Ironically, they both showed up at the house at the same time.

Richard said, "That bad, huh?"

Penelope said, "Yeeeaah, we had to leave. I called Kevin and he said we could sleep up at their house."

"Oh that was a good idea. Did you sleep well?"

"No, after talking to Marsha this morning, I forgot you're supposed to put their dogs in the kennel outside so they don't run around at night. Their dogs were in heaven chasing everything in sight and I listened to it all night, sheesh!"

Richard gave Penelope a hug and said, "Well, at least you're back safe and we can all sleep together tonight. Let's go out to dinner and then you, Tyler and me can look at houses tonight." With relief, Penelope said, "That would be great!"

Tyler said, "Yeahhh, more houses!"

They searched for houses and drove around until 11:00 p.m. In fact, they did that for the next couple of evenings. Tyler always fell asleep in the car and Richard and Penelope stared up at the moon and stars through the sunroof of their van talking together and praying that God would provide them with a new home.

When they returned home on one of the evenings from their house hunting, Penelope turned the upstairs hall light on from downstairs so she could see. She carried Tyler in her arms up the stairs and into their bedroom. She tucked Tyler into bed, and kissed him on his cheek. As she was leaving the bedroom the hall light started flickering. As it was flickering she heard an electrical static sound buzzing. Then the light started dimming to a brown color. This continued for a few minutes. She had the creepiest feeling and could sense that something was staring at her from the hallway. Her stomach had that queasy feeling again and she just froze, staring at the light. Logic took over in her mind. She thought, *you can't blame everything on a spiritual cause. Maybe there's a problem with the outlet or the city line.* She turned around and walked back into their bedroom, picked up the phone and called their neighbor, Tracy.

"Hey Tracy, its Penelope, are you guys having any problems with your power?"

Tracy said, "With our power? Uh, no our power is on. Why are you guys having problems?"

"Well, yeah, we have some lights flickering and dimming on and off."

"I don't know what to say, if you need anything call me back, okay?"

"Okay, thanks Tracy." Penelope went downstairs and told Richard that she'd called Tracy and they didn't have any problems with their electricity.

Richard said, "Wooooow, this house is really getting creepy." They both went to bed and as soon as they walked through the hallway back into their bedroom, the lights started flickering with that eerie static sound. It creeped them both out. Richard and Penelope tried to go to sleep but Penelope couldn't shake the feeling that "they" weren't done with their shenanigans. As she dozed off, she had this feeling of floating in the air and that a dark figure with an evil expression kept getting really close to her face. Every time the spirit did that, she would jump and wake up. When she woke up the third time, Richard was dreaming or thought he was. He kept moaning and kicking his legs like he was running. Penelope woke him up and he gasped, "That was the weirdest thing. I just felt like I was leaving my body and these evil spirits were trying to keep me from waking up. They were pulling on me."

Just as he finished explaining, they both felt hands that stroked down their back through the mattress!

Richard gasped and said, "Oh my gosh! Did you feel that?" Penelope immediately said,

"Yes... you get out in the name of Jesus." It was quiet for a second and then their bed was bumped into as if someone standing at the base of their bed had pushed it.

Richard said, "This house belongs to God and I command you leave, leave right now."

Penelope leaned over the bed and checked on Tyler and he was sound asleep. The room got quiet again, and then they heard their grandmother clock downstairs bonging out of whack again,

BOOONNNG, BING, BING, BANG BANG! They both were holding onto each other.

Richard said, "Don't worry; I'm not going downstairs tonight." Eventually they both were able to slowly fall back to sleep.

The next morning, Tyler woke up rested but his mom and dad were beat. Richard said, "We are *not* spending the night here tonight. I'm going to call my parents and see if we can go stay there. Are you okay with that, Penelope?"

She said, "Are you kidding me? That would be great! I think they would enjoy our company."

After Richard spoke with his parents, they were more than happy to have the three of them spend the night. It was Friday night, and the following day in his parent's town, they had a Saturday Market which would be fun to walk around and enjoy some breakfast and coffee. As soon as they arrived at Richard's parent's house, you could feel the peace within their home.

Richard whispered to Penelope, "Boy, what a difference here, huh?"

Penelope said, "I know, it feels good to be somewhere normal." She reached down and hugged Tyler because she was happy he was somewhere that would be peaceful for the night. Richard and Penelope were able to sleep in a bed together and they made a bed for Tyler on the floor out of comforters and pillows. Tyler snuggled up just fine; after all, he was used to sleeping by his mom and dad on his mattress at home anyway. Richard's parents lived right by the railroad tracks and in the middle of the night, their bed started shaking from a train. Penelope immediately thought it was something else, but Richard rolled toward her and said, "Don't worry, it's just the train."

They both snuggled together and slept wonderfully the rest of the night.

The next morning was so nice and relaxing. They all went to the Saturday market together. Richard's sister and her husband met them there. Penelope treated his sister to a cinnamon bun for her birthday. Tyler had fun running around with his granddad. He was a proud grandfather, walking Tyler around to meet all of his friends. It sure was a nice break from the house, plus the other three children would be returning the following week. Both Penelope and Richard were looking forward to having them back. Plus Penelope's mom and sister, Amber, would be visiting within two weeks. Penelope could not wait to see them and spend some quality time together.

The following week arrived and Michael was the first one back. He had a nice tan from visiting Florida and was so cute explaining his trip. There were all kinds of safari animals that they could watch from the window of their accommodations. Casey and Cassandra came walking through the door all excited to see everyone. They, too, had nice tans from their adventures in Michigan. It was a good time hearing stories, and Tyler loved having the family all together again. It was a very peaceful night's sleep for everyone, and Penelope thanked God.

It was time to prepare for Grand mom Carter and Aunt Amber to visit! Everyone was excited and helped Mom prepare the guest room for their grand mom and aunt to sleep in. Cassandra was nice enough to have Aunt Amber sleep in her room and grand mom slept in the spare bedroom downstairs. Cassandra slept on an extra mattress in the boy's room. Penelope was excited because they were staying at her house for the first four nights and then they would go up to her brother's house for the remainder of their stay. When they arrived, everyone was greeted by hugs and kisses. Amber walked up to Penelope and said, "If I see, hear or even smell those filthy varmints, they will be told to leave and they won't know *what* hit them."

Penelope started laughing and said, "It's about time we had some real warriors in this house. Listen up, if you have any problems in the night, don't worry because I'll already be up, missy." They both started laughing. That's exactly what got those two in trouble while growing up, they always were laughing and cutting up about something. Then Penelope's mom chimed in and said, "Well, I'll be downstairs all by my lonesome. Who's going to rescue me, huh? Poor little me."

Then they all three started laughing really hard. Penelope's mom lifted her chest up with pride and said, "Better yet, I've got the power of God behind me, girl, and I'll give them something to make them want to leave." Penelope said, "Give me an "Amen" sister in the *hooooooouuse*."

The next morning, Penelope anxiously awaited their report of how their evening went. She asked, "How did you guys sleep?"

Grand mom said, "Well, I was kind of disappointed that I didn't have to use God's power last night."

Amber said, "Then I guess I was the chosen one, because "they" came in a couple of times and I told them to leave and finally I got back to sleep."

"Sorry, Amber," Penelope said.

Amber said, "That's okay, hon, we knew you were having problems out here, so you know we're not going to let that keep us from visiting."

Penelope said, "Awww, thanks guys! I'm really happy that you're here."

"Are we going to look at houses with you guys today?" Amber asked.

Surprised, Penelope said, "Sure! If you guys want to. Obviously we aren't going to be doing that the whole time you're here,"

Amber said, "Well, we planned on looking with you and we don't care if that's all we do. We're here to support you guys, and mom and I feel that you will find the house that God wants you to have while we're here. So let's go find it!"

Excited, Penelope answered, "Like I said before, can I get an Amen from my sista?" They both started laughing. Mom said, "I can see it's going to be a long day for me."

After breakfast, everyone piled into the car to meet with their realtor at the first house. Their realtor planned on viewing a list of six homes that day. Once again, Tyler was excited and loved to go, the other three had fun too, but probably wouldn't last as long. All the houses were beautiful but only one caught Richard and Penelope's attention. This house was beautiful on the inside and out and was very, very peaceful. The only downside was that the backyard had a very steep hill and Penelope was envisioning her two active boys falling or rolling down the hill and hitting their head on something. It had a beautiful pond and patio but too bad the rest of the yard was not level. The garage had plenty of room for Richard's work samples and there was a separate shop perfect for Penelope's decorating business. They both were talking about it and thought maybe they could fill-in and level the yard. After Richard really thought about it, he figured the cost would be too high. The access to the backyard would be very difficult for trucks to enter or grading to be done. Mom leaned over to Penelope and said, "This house is very nice and it does have good energy here. It's peaceful."

Penelope said, "I know mom but the yard is bothering me a little."

Her mom said, "I'm not sure if this is the one or not. We'll have to pray about it."

That was the last home to view from the list. It was time to get back home and fix lunch for everyone. Mom and Amber planned on driving up to their brother's house for lunch and say hi to them. They would come back that afternoon. In the meantime, Richard said he had been looking around earlier in the week and discovered a small development close by. "Do you want to go look?" he said.

Penelope said, "Well, the kids have to go to the bathroom and I'm really tired."

With hope in his voice, Richard said, "We could just drive by?"

"Okay, let's drive by."

Cassandra said, "Can we hurry, I really have to go to the bathroom."

"Hang in there honey, its close by," her mom said.

They drove up the cul-de-sac and there were a few homes already finished and the two that were being worked on were the ones for sale.

Richard said, "I was thinking about the yellow house. Are you sure you don't want to look?"

Penelope said, "Wow, that's really nice. I kind of do but the kids are getting antsy and hungry. Sorry, hon."

"That's okay we'll stop by another day. Do you like it though?"

Excited, Penelope said, "Yes, I really do like it; it's pretty." So they turned around and went back to their house.

The rest of the visit with mom and Amber was a lot of fun. They were able to go to a festival in the gorge, have lunch in a western restaurant, hike at Angel Mountain and just spend time with each other. Since Penelope's dad passed away, her mom was going to have an in-law suite built next to her sister, Leslie's house back East. She was in the middle of selling their home in Pennsylvania. During their stay, grand mom's realtor had called and said she had an offer on her house! It was exciting for everyone and the realtor just happened to be their cousin. It was nice for a relative to assist Mom with the whole process of selling. Their cousin faxed the offer over on Richard's fax machine and Mom was able to sign it and get the contract going. We all celebrated that night with the whole family.

The next day it was time for grand mom and Aunt Amber to go. It was really hard to say goodbye to them, but they had to get back home. Penelope and Richard and all of the kids drove them to the airport. They were able to drop them off at the front doors of the airport and say their goodbyes there.

Mom said to Penelope, "I really thought we were going to help you guys find your house. I guess we were just here to help you by praying and supporting you."

Penelope said, "Awww, thanks mom. That's okay, God will show us. I'm just really happy we were able to spend some time together and have some laughs."

Mom hugged Richard and said, "You're doing a great job with my daughter and your family, thank you. We love you, Richard."

He gave her a big hug and said, "I love you too." All the kids hugged them both goodbye and then mom and Amber walked into the airport.

New House

Richard said, "Hey Penelope, remember that house we drove by while your mom was here?"

"Oh yeah!" she said. "Do you want to go by there right now with the kids and take a look?"

"Sure!" They drove back to the house and the builders were still working on it. It wasn't quite finished but they could walk through and take a look around.

When they walked up, the owner approached them and said, "Are you here to take a look at the house?"

Richard said, "If that's okay with you guys."

Penelope said, "Hey! We know you. Oh my gosh, what a small world."

The couple that was selling the home had other homes for sale in the past that Richard and Penelope had looked at just for fun. Plus this lady's husband used to ride the same bus Penelope did when she worked in downtown Portland. So they kind of knew each other already. Greta and Sam were their names.

Greta said, "I just asked God to find a buyer for this home! "We haven't advertised these homes yet. You should know these homes are built by Christian people. Well, go ahead and take a look around, just make sure your kids are careful around the debris and stuff."

"Okay, great," Richard said. Everyone walked in and took a look around. It definitely was a "wow" house. All the kids ran upstairs and decided who was going to get what bedroom. Richard and Penelope glanced at each other the whole time and were really impressed.

Richard said, "Do you like it?"

"I love it, the laundry room is much smaller, and I'm not sure where the pantry is."

Greta came in and said, "What do you think?"

Penelope said, "We love it, but I'm concerned about the pantry. Where is the pantry?"

Greta said, "Oh, everything is built right into the cabinets."

Greta opened the doors to the cabinets and showed Penelope that one half of the kitchen cabinets consisted of the pantry and the other half were for storage. "Wow! I love how it's all compact with pullouts and built-ins."

Richard said, "Let's go look at the other house and compare." So they all walked over to the house next door to see what the floor plan was like in that home. It was a very nice home too, but the bedrooms were split up in the house. The Master bedroom was on the main level, two bedrooms were upstairs and they needed three. It did have a basement large enough to create another bedroom down there, but then everyone would be scattered. So everyone trooped back to the other house and looked around again. They told Greta and Sam that they would think about it and took their number to contact them.

After leaving, Richard said, "I think we should buy it."

Penelope said, "If we do, I guess we could make it contingent upon us selling our existing home."

"Of course, we couldn't do it any other way. Why don't we call them tomorrow and walk through it again, but tonight we're going to pray and see if this is where God wants us to be."

The next day they walked through the house again, this time without the kids so they could think and focus on what God wanted them to do. They called their realtor to see what a good offer would be and to see if there were any bites on their existing home. The good news from their realtor was to offer about $10,000 less than the advertised price and the bad news was there were no offers on the existing home. They discussed it with Greta and she said she would take their offer but not contingent upon their selling their home.

Greta said, "I can't take the risk of this house sitting on hold for several months when I could probably sell it faster than that."

Richard was not happy with that at all. Penelope stood there and prayed to herself. She had this overwhelming peace that this was the home for them. Greta let them talk among themselves in private.

Penelope said to Richard, "You know what? You're not going to like what I have to say, but you need to listen to me, okay?"

Richard looked up and said in a curt tone, "What?"

Ignoring his tone, Penelope continued, "Okay, I believe that God really wants us to step out in faith and trust that he will take care of the other house. I think we should move in here as soon as we can. It's not the 'normal' thing to do but if we stay in that house any longer, I'm afraid of what will happen to you and Tyler."

Richard responded, "I know we need to move out. You're right, Penelope, I can't stay any longer, I'm going nuts and they *are* after Tyler. I'm just not comfortable handling it that way. We're going to have two house payments for a while and I'm not sure we can handle that. Do you understand where I'm coming from?"

"Yes Richard I do, I do, hon. Just make sure you're not putting God in a box. You need to let go of all of that and trust in him and I really believe that's what he wants us to do. After praying last night and right now, I don't see another way out."

They both were quiet for a few seconds and then Richard said, "Penelope, why do you always have to be right?" Richard took a deep breath and then paused for a few seconds. "Okay, let's do it," he said. "We need to get out of the other house and quickly." They both were relieved and excited. Penelope could see that this was going to be tough on Richard but she totally believed that God would make a way.

Sure enough, the contracts went through and they had to sign a bridge loan in order to use the equity in their existing home to purchase the new home. The bridge loan was at a higher interest rate than your typical home loan. This type of loan also required higher payments that increased as the home sat on the market until it sold. This was a *huge* leap of faith for Richard and Penelope.

They had to wait about two weeks before moving in. In the meantime, Greta called them one day and said, "Why don't you guys come over during the evening and check out your house? You really need to see it at night, it's beautiful."

They decided to do that, as it gave them an excuse to get out of the other house for a while. When they arrived, Greta had snacks in the cupboards for the kids and gave Richard and Penelope the key to lock up after they were finished looking around.

Greta was smiling. As she left, she said, "Enjoy."

"Unbelievable!" Richard said. "Who let's someone walk through the house again at night before they move in. This is great!"

Penelope said, "Well, this is definitely from God for us to see how peaceful it is here during the night." They all walked through the house, loving every minute of it. Penelope went upstairs and turned all the lights off and walked through, praying and asking God to show her if there was anything to be concerned about. There was nothing but pure peace and serenity. She just stood there enjoying the peaceful moment in the dark hallway. All of the kids walked upstairs to see where their mom was; they didn't mind that the lights were off. Oh how Penelope and Richard wished that they could all sleep there that night.

It was a week before moving day and it was time to have their estate sale. Everything was moved into the garage with the exception of some larger pieces of furniture. It was a great turnout and a lot of their things were sold at face value. They did have a surprise customer--- their pastor's wife from their previous church that had the prayer group come over. Michelle was her name and she was always so laid back and nice. Any garage sale that Penelope had gone to, you could always count on seeing Michelle there. She walked up and greeted them.

Richard said, "Oh, hi Michelle, we're having some really good deals here today. Feel free to look around."

Other customers started pouring in as well and the weather couldn't have been better. Penelope was inside when someone knocked at the front door, so she went and answered it. Penelope said, "Hi, Michelle, good to see you here."

"You too, do you mind if I have a look around upstairs?"

Penelope said, "Oh, no not at all, feel free to browse around all you like."

She walked slowly up the stairs and Penelope watched her reach the top. Then she walked out into the garage to see if Richard needed any help. After five minutes or so, Michelle came back downstairs and was looking for Penelope. She found her out on the front porch and started talking softly to her, "You know Frank and I had some spiritual experiences at our other home too. We think it was some music that was brought into our home that was not of God. You know music like the really hard rock stuff. It didn't happen all of the time, but every once in a while we had experiences that we would have to pray about and then it would leave for awhile and come back again. We have since moved from that home, *but* that's not why we left. I guess what I'm saying is that we can relate to you having problems here and I understand."

She placed her hand on Penelope's arm gently and said, "We'll see ya." Richard came back inside and asked Penelope what Michelle had said. Penelope filled him in on the conversation and Richard said, "Wow, so she gets it! She understands what's going on here, right?"

Penelope said, "Yes, she does. She may not know the scope of it all but what matters is that she was able to relate."

Richard said, "Then that means when she went upstairs she must have sensed something." "She definitely did or she wouldn't have spoken to me in a reassuring way."

It was finally moving day, and they could not get out of there fast enough. Since their home was still up for sale, they left behind some items to stage the home so it wouldn't be totally empty. It was fun unpacking in their brand new home and having the kids get settled into their new bedrooms. They all four loved the new house. Tyler really improved at the new house. He was able to sleep without interruptions or waking up in the middle of the night. He was comfortable in his own bedroom all by himself.

While the kids were in school and Richard was working, Penelope had to go back to the other house and stage everything in the hopes of selling it quickly. Every time she was in there working, she felt like she was being watched. Richard barely went over there to help but Penelope totally understood because it was more emotionally draining and stressful for Richard. Penelope had painters come in and neutralize the entire house with one paint color, which made it look very nice and uniform. The dishwasher broke, so they had to replace it with a new one, and the family room carpet was really worn down so that was replaced as well. So the staging was finally completed. It all actually turned out very nice and the realtor was impressed. However, they were not impressed with their realtor at all. It just seemed as if none of their realtors were very motivated to sell for them.

Shortly after they moved into their new home, the vision Penelope had just a few months earlier about Michael's mom moving had come about. Michael's mom had placed their home up for sale and it was a Windermere "For Sale" sign on their lawn just as in her vision! It was weird, they didn't even move too far from their existing home. The home sold very fast, which was not surprising because their home was very unique and quaint. After many prayers, God had mended the relationship between Richard's ex-wife and Richard and Penelope. This was good as they could contact her not just for their realtor information, but important things for Michael as well. Richard and Penelope were able to get a hold of their realtor in hopes that the agent could sell their existing home as swiftly. Their realtor came over the next day and discussed pricing and so forth and they had their home listed once again with a new realtor. This realtor had a really good reputation so hope was rekindled.

Four months passed and still no bites on the house! Richard was beginning to get stressed out since they were paying two of everything, mortgages, insurance, taxes, utility bills and the list went on. Penelope needed to travel back and forth at least once a week or once every two weeks to check on the house and clean it every once in awhile. The only good thing was that it didn't require much cleaning at all.

Penelope had a long talk with God. She and Richard were totally thankful and relieved to be out of that wicked house, but somehow they couldn't let go of it totally just because of the concern for other people or families that would move in after them. She had prayed to God to bring them finalization and to release the spiritual hold over that house through the power of God and the Holy Spirit.

That very night, Casey had a very powerful spiritual dream. Casey was dreaming that he and his friends were playing a game at the other house and they were in his bedroom closet. When they tried to get out of the closet, they couldn't get the door to open. Inside of the closet on the wall was a circle that opened up in a swirling pattern which then became a three dimensional large black hole. He said that in his dream, his mom tried to cover the hole up with paint, and every time she tried to cover up the hole, it would come back. He and his friends finally got out of the house and they were trying to run away. He woke up when they were running.

Richard and Penelope decided to take Casey over to the other house to pray together. They anointed each other beforehand and asked God to reveal to them what this all meant. All three held hands and prayed in a circle on the floor of Casey's old bedroom. When they were finished praying, Penelope opened the door of his closet and examined all of the walls, thinking there may have been something she missed before when she was searching for clues. She even brought sandpaper to rough away the paint, thinking maybe something was underneath, some kind of sign or symbol. There wasn't anything. The three of them sat down together on the carpet again and Penelope started to pray, "God, please show us what Casey's dream means. What are we missing? Do you want us to do anything while we're here?" They sat there quietly waiting for God to answer for so long that Richard fell asleep. Casey was ready to go home but Penelope was willing to wait until they received a direct answer. They never did while they were there, but after about a week of focusing on God, Penelope received an answer! It became clear what Casey's dream really meant. It went off in her head like a light bulb. She was so excited. She ran into Casey's room and said, "I know what your dream means!"

Before she even gave Casey a chance to speak, she said, "It means that no matter what we say or do, those spirits are not going to leave!"

Casey said, "Yeah mom, that makes more sense than what we did, sandpapering the closet wall."

She answered, "I know, I just wanted to make sure we did everything possible to eradicate those evil boogers."

Casey said, "Mom, I love you and you're doing a really good job."

"Awww, thanks Casey" They hugged each other and Mom gave him a kiss on his cheek.

Four more months passed…

Richard had received several phone messages from Pastor Frank.

Richard said, "I don't know, Penelope. I feel funny calling him back."

"Why?" she asked.

"It's been almost a year since we attended his church and it's going to be awkward."

Penelope said, "You need to call him back and find out what he wants. I think it has everything to do with the house and how it was handled by his staff."

Richard said, "Then maybe you should call him."

She said, "He's calling you, not me."

"Well, I can't take it anymore. I'm stressed out! You walk around here like life is grand and nothing is wrong. We have bills coming in left and right and I can't keep paying them! You're not the one paying the bills, I am!"

There was a long pause and then Penelope said in a gentle loving voice, "God has provided for us; that's why I walk around here like that. No matter what, I believe he will sell the house when he's good and ready. We could have lost both homes if not for him blessing your business. Think about it, no matter how many bills you have coming in, we are not struggling, Richard. It could be a lot worse! You and Tyler are out of that house, Tyler is sleeping great, and is at peace here. Do not put God in a box. By the way, I love you and we will be fine; everything will work out great, you'll see."

The next day Penelope prayed about calling Pastor Frank because she knew Richard couldn't handle that right now. When she was praying the phone rang and on the caller ID was Pastor Frank's number. Penelope's heart started beating fast and she reached for the phone and then felt like she couldn't pick it up. She wished Richard would deal with this because Pastor Frank really wanted to speak with him. The phone stopped ringing and Cassandra came running down to the kitchen where her mom was with the phone in her hand.

"Mom, it's Pastor Frank," and she handed her mom the phone, Penelope took a deep breath and asked God to give her the words to speak to him. Then she took the phone.

"Hi, Pastor Frank."

"Hey Penelope, how are you?"

"We're doing great!"

He asked, "Are you?"

With confidence she answered, "Yes, we are."

"How come?"

"Well, we moved and it's been absolutely wonderful at our new house. It's full of nothing but peace."

Pastor Frank said, "That's really good to hear, that's kind of why I'm calling. I've been trying to get a hold of Richard, but I will tell you instead since I have you on the phone."

"Sorry about that, Pastor Frank. He has been traveling and is under stress about selling the other house."

"Well, I can understand that. I've been meaning to call you guys sooner but I wanted to let you know I'm really sorry about dropping the ball with your other house. I also know that the prayer group did not handle things the best way that they could have."

"Well, no offense, Pastor Frank, but I was really surprised that they would require Richard to accept the Holy Spirit when they were supposed to be there to battle for us."

"I know and that's why I'm calling. I had a lot going on in my life. I don't know if you knew that or not, but that's no excuse and I'm asking you to forgive me. Hopefully you and your family will come back home to our church, we miss you."

Penelope paused as her negative feelings literally melted away and from her heart she said, "Pastor Frank, we forgive you. We also understand that not everyone knows or has the capacity to handle the situation that we were in, but perhaps our church could educate itself regarding future scenarios that may come up. We do miss your church a lot. We have been going to a different church, but it's not the same at all. We didn't know you had anything going on in your life that was challenging."

"It doesn't matter. What's more important is that we try to make it right with you and Richard and get you guys back to your home church where you belong."

Penelope felt much peace from their conversation; it was a relief and blessing all at once. "Pastor Frank, thanks so much for calling and I will be sure to tell Richard that you did so."

Pastor Frank said, "Okay! We look forward to seeing you guys in church this Sunday, bye bye."

Penelope hung up and started to cry. It felt so good to clear all of that up. She could not wait to call Richard and tell him. She had to leave a message on his cell phone to call her back instead. As she waited for him to call back, she thanked God for using Cassandra to pick up the phone and speak with Pastor Frank. Penelope went upstairs and thanked Cassandra for answering the phone.

Cassandra said, "I knew it was Pastor Frank and that you were supposed to talk with him, Mom."

"Cassandra! God has used you again" and she gave her daughter a big hug and kissed her on her cheek. Richard finally called back. "Guess what, Richard!?"

"What?"

"Guess who called?"

"Who?"

"Pastor Frank."

"Really?!"

"Guess who spoke with him?"

"No way, tell me all about it." After explaining everything in detail to Richard, he said, "We are definitely going to church on Sunday. Good job, Penelope."

She said "Thank you, hon. I still think he would like to speak with you, though."

Richard said, "Well, maybe we'll be able to on Sunday. I have to go though, I saw that you called and thought maybe it was important, which it was. I'll see you later."

"Okay hon, bye."

Sunday morning came around and the whole family was kind of excited to go back to their church. They all walked through the doors and felt peaceful and relieved at the same time. Pastor Frank made a point to come up to Richard and he hugged everyone. He and Richard spoke very briefly.

Afterwards, Penelope said to Richard, "That was a quick conversation."

Richard said, "Do you remember that really funny speaker, Jerry Cook?"

"Oh yes, I do."

"Well, Pastor Frank told me that he had mentioned our situation to him and wanted his advice."

Anxious to hear, she asked, "What did he say?"

"He said that if he were in our shoes, then he would leave too-- that it's a no brainer."

Surprised, Penelope said, "Really?! That confirms that we did the right thing. God's hand has been on this all along."

They all sat down in the sanctuary, and as Pastor Frank began his sermon, he looked over at Richard and Penelope and mouthed the words, "Welcome home," with a big smile on his face. After the service was over, a friend of Richard's came over to him and said, "Hey, it's good to see you guys here."

Richard said, "It's good to be here, thanks."

"You know, if I were in your position with your house situation, I would do what's best for my family no matter what people here at church say. God tells us to take care of our families and if something like that does not leave, then you protect your loved ones."

Richard said, "Thanks, man, that means a lot that you would tell us that." They gave each other a man hug.

On Monday morning, it was time for Penelope to check on the other house again. On the way over, Penelope pulled off the side of the road that faced the back of the house. She got out of the car and stood there looking into the back yard. She was praying and asking God in her mind, why haven't these evil spirits left? Why are they allowed to stay? We know you have the ultimate power to eradicate and destroy them. So she stood there for a few minutes and waited upon the Lord for her answer. As she stood there, she literally could hear drums pounding a steady beat; they sounded like Indian drums. The drums started to get louder and louder and were accompanied by Indian chanting. In her mind she could see blood coming up out of the ground in the back yard by their pond. It seemed very symbolic of what took place on that property many, many years ago. She then asked God, what would it take to be able to have the property blessed? He showed her fire everywhere surrounding the house. The house was not on fire, but the land was. It was very clear to her that it never had anything to do with the house; it was always the land. Her memories of their neighbor coming over, explaining about the boy who lived there previously and the way his mother acted during the inspection all flashed before her. She then realized they were given signs all along, they just never saw them.

When she arrived back at their new house, Greta came over to speak with her. Greta and her husband had moved into the house next door to Richard and Penelope because they couldn't sell it. Greta asked Penelope, "Have you had any luck selling your other home yet?"

She said, "No, it's been twelve months and no bites, just little nibbles."

"You might want to call this other realtor we're familiar with. He's really nice and good at what he does. Plus he's a Christian so that would be beneficial too. I'll give you his number."

Penelope said, "That would be great, thanks!"

Penelope gave the realtor a call and he came right over to their new house to fill out all of the paperwork. He explained in detail how he felt the market would flow in the coming months and what to expect. How quickly a customer would like their house to move is determined upon how much they're willing to sell it for and how long they're willing to wait. So the next step is for the customer to sort out those facts and decide on a price. After all of the realtors they'd dealt with and a market that had crashed, Penelope felt best to set it at a price to get it off their laps at $450,000. The realtor agreed with the price range as well. He then went over to their other house by himself and set up his signs, etc....

In the meantime at their new house, Penelope unpacked some more boxes from the garage and carried them up to the bonus room. While she was unpacking them in the bonus room, she felt the presence of her dad again. He came in very peacefully and with a bright light around him.

Penelope said, "Hi dad, I miss you."

"Hi daughter, listen, I don't have a lot of time to talk with you this time. I'm busy helping God. He wants me to tell you that you need to write a book about the other house and it's to be called, 'Enlightened Within.' This book will reach a lot of people; you have no idea. It will be used as a tool to help those in similar situations. You will be used in a mighty way."

Surprised by his message, Penelope said, "Thanks dad, I will write it."

Her dad said, "I have to go now."

She said, "I love you dad!"

"Love you too, daughter. I'm proud of you." Penelope watched her father leave through the window of the bonus room. She could feel his happiness but at the same time it made her sad because she missed him so much. After a few minutes of digesting the message received, she felt better and ran downstairs to tell Richard what just happened. Richard was surprised but totally agreed that the book should be written.

Two months later…

One week before Christmas, Richard was working in the garage and Penelope was in the kitchen fixing coffee. A fax came through in Richard's office and it was an offer for the other house! The offer was for $445,000, which was very reasonable, as it was listed at $450,000. Everything was in place; they just had to agree and sign their offer! Penelope took the paper in her hand and ran to the garage. As she stood in the doorway, she started to cry.

Richard said, "What's wrong now?!"

She could barely get her words out, it was so unbelievable. "We got an offer on the house."

Richard came over, looked at the paper and they both started to cry together. They hugged each other. They pulled slightly away from one another and stared into each other's eyes with joy and relief. In unison they said, "Thank you God… thank you and Merry Christmas!"

Epilogue

The McCallisters clearly lived on cursed land. It is very common knowledge that small towns scattered along the Columbia River Gorge on both Washington and Oregon sides have been cursed by American Indians. Occult activities in this region are alleged to be among the strongest in the United States.

The lesson learned from the McCallister story is that we as Christians should always pray about every decision we make, no matter how great or small they may seem. By praying first, we are allowing God's spirit to influence and guide our daily decisions and activities.

God chose not to remove the spiritual conflict within their home though the family was protected from harm. As we all know, God doesn't always reveal to us everything. He has the perfect plan and sometimes we just need to have faith. This family became much closer to God, and that's an important lesson in this particular story.

If you really want to have a huge positive impact on this world, there are three things that you need to trust and believe in:

1) God (believe his Word)
2) Jesus (God's only Son sent here on earth to die for our sins)

3) Holy Spirit (the <u>living</u> power of God)

These three powerful persons work together as a team. God created this earth and all the people. He then sent his Son, Jesus to die for our sins because we couldn't do it alone. The Holy Spirit is our spiritual battery so to speak. The Holy Spirit is the Power of God.

When you ask God to listen to your prayers and you ask for forgiveness of your sins (we all sin everyday) also ask the Holy Spirit to empower you and guide you. Your life will not remain the same. You will be equipped with the tools to conquer whatever obstacles this world will throw at you and when times are good, you will be able to bathe in the sunlight.

Made in the USA
Lexington, KY
22 June 2016